designing with models

designing with models

A Studio Guide to Making and Using Architectural Design Models

CRISS B. MILLS

John Wiley & Sons, Inc.
New York • Chichester • Weinheim • Brisbane • Singapore • Toronto

Copyright © 2000 by Criss Mills. All rights reserved.

Published by John Wiley & Sons, Inc.

Published simultaneously in Canada.

This publication is designed to provide accurate and authoritative information in regard to the subject matter covered. It is sold with the understanding that the publisher is not engaged in rendering professional services. If professional advice or other expert assistance is required, the services of a competent professional person should be sought.

Library of Congress Cataloging-in-Publication Data:
Mills, Criss.
    Designing with models : a studio guide to making and using
architectural design models / Criss Mills.
        p.   cm.
    "Published simultaneously in Canada"—T.p. verso.
    Includes bibliographical references and index.
    ISBN 0-471-34589-X (paper : acid-free paper)
    1. Architectural models Handbooks, manuals, etc.   I. Title.
NA2790.M5 2000
720'.22'8—dc21   99-26957

Printed in the United States of America.

10 9 8 7 6 5 4

CONTENTS

FOREWORD

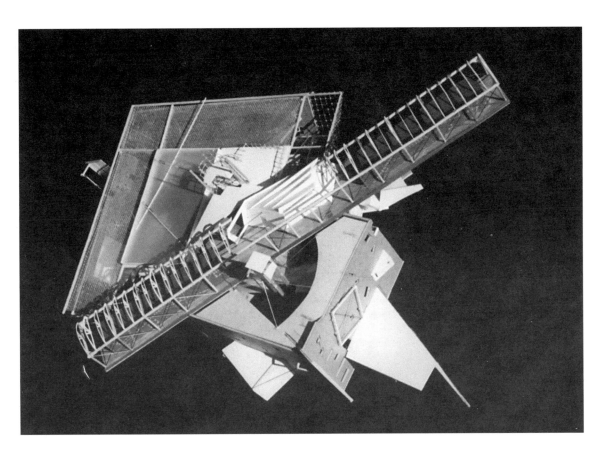

This book is about using the architectural model as a tool for discovery. When used as an integral part of the design process, study models are capable of generating information in an amount of time comparable to that needed for drawing, and they offer one of the strongest exploration methods available.

The strategies, assembly techniques, and step-by-step illustrations presented here, which were developed over years of model exploration, provide a broad range of options.

Because this book is primarily concerned with the design process, elaborate presentation models, typically built after a design is completed, are not addressed. Instead, work is explored with quick-sketch constructions and simple finish models that can be built with materials suitable for studio or in-house construction.

Although most of the projects are approached from an architectural perspective, the techniques apply equally well to three-dimensional artwork and commercial designs.

designing with models

START

Equipment, Materials, and Model Types

This chapter includes the basic equipment and definitions needed to prepare for modeling. Although an effort has been made to employ common terms, in the absence of industry-wide standardization, alternate or overlapping definitions may be encountered in different studio settings.

The equipment and materials presented in this chapter are appropriate to basic study models. For additional information on materials and equipment, see Chapters 5 and 7.

Equipment

The equipment used for most modeling needs is divided into two sets.

Basic Equipment

This equipment can be very simple and is adequate for most modeling tasks.

Expanded Equipment

This equipment can make the job easier and help with specialized tasks. For additional equipment, see Chapters 5 and 7.

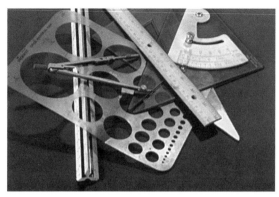

Drafting Tools
A set of common drawing tools used to lay out the model parts.

X-Acto Knife and No. 11 Blades
The primary knife. Keep knife sharp with frequent blade changes. Blades are most economically purchased in packs of 100.

Steel Ruler
The primary cutting edge. The ruler should have a nonslip cork backing. For economy, a wooden ruler with a metal edge can be used. Avoid aluminum rulers as they will dull knife blades very quickly.

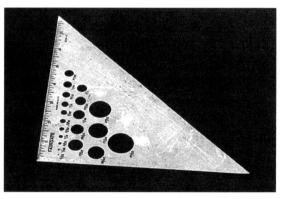

Metal Triangle
Used for right-angle cuts and drafting with a knife. Unfortunately, most metal triangles are made of aluminum, but plastic triangles with steel edges can be found at some suppliers.

Scissors

For quick study models and editing cuts.

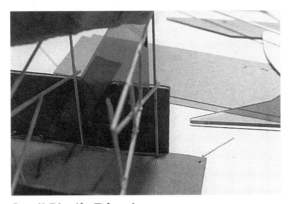

Small Plastic Triangle

Used to square and level model parts for accurate assembly.

Hot Glue Gun

For quick assembly and hard-to-glue materials like metal. Can be very messy and is not well suited for finish work.

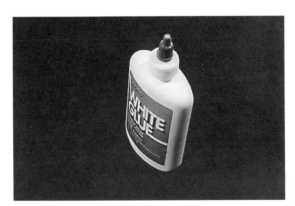

White Glue

The primary adhesive. Used to attach most paper materials. When applied properly, white glue dries quickly but allows for disassembly for experimentation.

Acetate Adhesive

Used for Plexiglas. A drop on the end of a knife blade can be applied by dragging the blade along the edge of the Plexiglas.

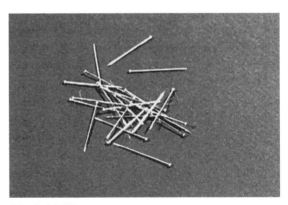

Straight Pins

Used to attach parts while glue is setting. Pins can be pulled, set for reinforcement, or cut off with side cutters.

Artists' Spray Adhesive
Used for attaching paper surfaces that will buckle with white glue. A very light coat on plans allows them to be used as templates. Avoid hardware store adhesive sprays, as they are too strong for this use.

Matte Knife
For cutting very thick materials. The blade thickness on this tool is not suited for fine work.

Small Metal and Plastic Triangles
Can be used to align model parts for gluing and for making accurate modification cuts directly on the model.

Drafting Tape
Used to attach parts while glue is setting. Avoid masking tape, as it will tear paper surfaces.

Small Scale Rule with End Cut Off
Used for taking measurements directly from the model. A scale can be drawn on a wooden stick to serve the same purpose.

Needle Nose Pliers
Used for delicate work and as an inexpensive third hand.

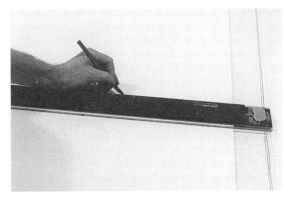

Steel Edge Parallel Bar
Makes cutting parts much faster. Useful for manufacturing multiple pieces of the same pattern.

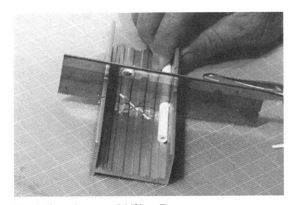

Modeling Saw and Miter Box
Used for clean cuts on small blocks and rods, as well for as angle cuts.

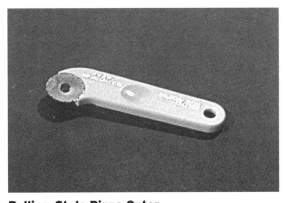

Rolling-Style Pizza Cuter
Used for transferring drawing lines to modeling surfaces. Roll cutter along lines to leave traces in modeling material. Cutters with pointed edges work best.

Sandpaper
Sandpaper can be used to level and remove the burrs from cuts.

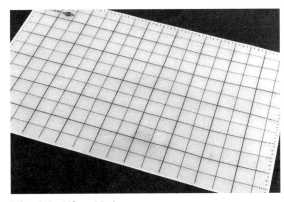

Vinyl Cutting Mat
Used to save drawing board surfaces.

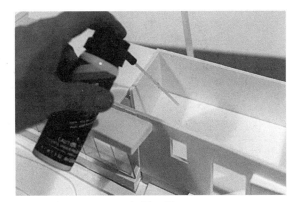

Canned Compressed-Air Cleaner
For cleaning dust off models. Works well for hard-to-reach inside corners.

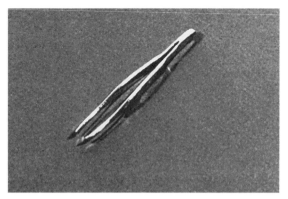

Tweezers
Used to handle delicate parts.

Electric Drill and Small Bits
Used for gang drilling multistory column holes in floor plates and other special holes.

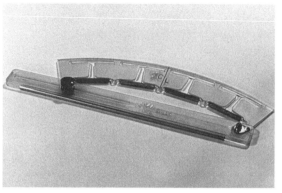

Acu Arc
Used for drafting smooth scaled curves.

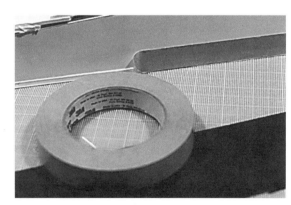

Double-Faced Transfer Tape
Used to attach paper; without the buckling tendencies of white glue.

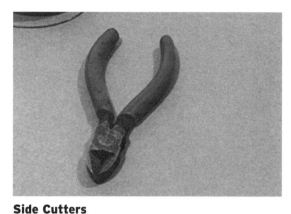

Side Cutters
For cutting pins and wire.

Soldering Gun
For soldering copper and steel wire. *Note:* Use rosin core solder.

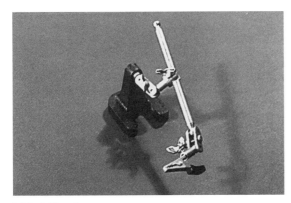

Third Hand
Helps hold parts for gluing, drying, and other tasks.

Soldering Iron
A soldering iron is an inexpensive alternative to a soldering gun. Small irons like this one produce comparatively little heat. They can be used by waiting longer for materials to heat up.

Materials

The following section describes the basic materials used for the majority of modeling tasks. Many choices are available; however, for the purpose of this book, the primary focus is on inexpensive, easily manipulated paperboard materials. See Chapters 5 and 7 for additional materials.

MATERIAL CONSIDERATIONS

- The speed with which the model is to be built

- The degree of modification and experimenting desired

- The ability of a material to hold its shape or span at scale modeling distances

- The thickness of the scaled component the model is intended to reflect

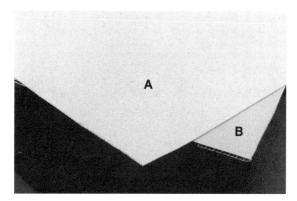

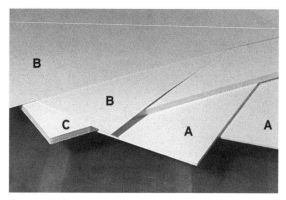

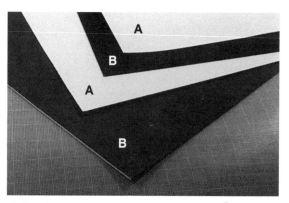

A—Gray Chipboard

- Available in two or four ply
- Inexpensive
- Cuts easily
- Spans moderately
- Thicker plies hard to cut
- Rougher finish
- Interesting alternative to white boards

B—Corrugated Cardboard

- Sheets are usually ⅛ in. thick
- Rough finish
- Interesting alternative
- Inexpensive and cuts easily
- Spans larger spaces well
- Reflects material thickness of midsize-to-larger models
- Can mock textured surface if top layer is removed

A—Foam Core

- Available in 1/16, ⅛, 3/16, ½ in. thicknesses
- Finished in appearance
- Cuts easily
- Suitable for large scales
- Can be matched to scale thickness

B—White Museum Board (Strathmore)

- Available in two-, four-, five-, and six-ply thicknesses
- Finished in appearance
- Relatively expensive
- Easy to cut
- Thinner plies not suitable for large spans

C—Gatorboard

- A thick, tough board similar to foam core
- Used primarily for model bases
- Finished in appearance
- Very difficult to cut

A—Poster paper

- Similar to thin museum board
- Inexpensive
- Available at drug and office supply stores
- Reasonably finished in appearance
- Suitable for small models
- Easy to cut
- Spans poorly

B—Colored Matte Board

- Similar to four-ply chipboard
- Takes several passes to cut
- Spans well
- Used for coding and contrast
- Edges should be mitered at 45 degrees on nonintegral color board

Note: With integral color board, color goes all the way through and should be used if possible. The exposed white edges of nonintegral color board severely degrade model appearance.

Plastic and Wood Modeling Sticks
Available in square and rectangular balsa or basswood shapes.

Plastic and Wood Dowels
Available in a variety of sizes and lengths.

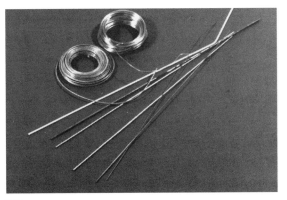

Wire
- White plastic coated wire
- Copper, steel, and aluminum roll
- Straight modeling wire

Clear Plastic and Plexiglas Sheets
- Used for glass simulation
- Available as thin Plexiglas from suppliers, at hobby shops, and as inexpensive picture framing sheets; avoid thin acetate sheets

White Graphic Art Tape
- Used for mullion simulation
- $\frac{1}{32}$ in. wide and smaller

Sewing Thread
Can be used to simulate cable lines or thin rods in tension.

Plastic Mylar
Mylar drafting sheets can be easily cut and used for curved translucent panels.

Enamel Spray Paint
- Used to paint models and wood rods.
- Automobile primer can be used as an under-coat on cardboard to prevent buckling.

Cloth and Trace
Drawing trace or light cloth can be used to fill in planes and simulate translucent membranes. Membranes can be curved and warped as needed.

Model Types

Models are referred to in a variety of ways, and terms may often be used interchangeably in different settings. Although there is no standard, the definitions in the following lists are commonly used.

All of the model types discussed (sketch, massing, development, etc.) are considered to be study models, including those used for formal presentations. As such, their purpose is to generate design ideas and serve as vehicles for refinement. They can range from quick, rough constructions to resolved models. Whatever state they are in, the term *study model* implies that they are always open to investigation and refinement.

Study models can be considered to belong to either of two groups. For the purposes of this discussion they are referred to as *primary models* and *secondary models*. The primary set has to do with the level or stage of design evolution, and the secondary set refers to particular sections or aspects of the project under focus. A secondary model type may be built as a primary model type, depending on the level of focus. For example, a model used to develop interior spaces would be thought of as an interior model but would also be a sketch model, development model, or presentation model, depending on its level of focus.

Primary Models

Primary models are abstract in concept and are employed to explore different stages of focus.

Sketch

Diagram

Concept

Massing

Solid/Void

Development

Presentation/Finish

Secondary Models

Secondary models are used to look at particular building or site components.

Site contour

Site context

Entourage/Site Foliage

Interior

Section

Facade

Framing/Structure

Detail/Connections

Sketch Models

Sketch models constitute the initial phase of study models. They are like the three-dimensional equivalent to drawing and sketching—a medium for speed and spontaneity.

Sketch models generally are not overly concerned with craft, but provide a quick way to visualize space. They are intended to be cut into and modified as exploration proceeds. These models may also be produced as a quick series to explore variations on a general design direction.

Although many of the models shown throughout this book are produced as expressive explorations, sketch models are also valuable when built with greater precision and used to explore formal qualities of alignment, proportion, and spatial definition.

Sketch models are generally built at relatively small scales from inexpensive materials such as chipboard or poster board.

Several examples of sketch models are shown, ranging from small building propositions to ideas exploring space, site relationships and formally aligned proportions.

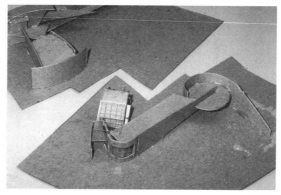

Sketch Model
Small alternative sketches can be made early in the design phase to explore basic building organizations and reflect general relationships of program circulation and architectural concerns (actual size, 4 in.).

Sketch Model
Sketch models can explore basic relationships between a number of program components (actual size, 11 in.).

Sketch Model
Sketch models can carry genetic information about the way building spaces will flow and read. In this case the model was a translation of drawing exercises that began incorporating the program (actual size, 6 in.).

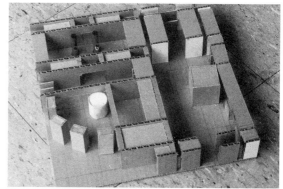

Sketch Model
Sketch models can explore formal alignments and controlled proportional readings (actual size, 11 in.).

Diagram Models

Diagrams models are related to sketch models and conceptual models; however, like their two-dimensional counterparts they map out abstract issues of program, structure, circulation, and site relationships.

Although they are similar to drawn forms, the three-dimensional quality of diagram models can begin to describe space as it relates to architectural issues and can suggest ideas for further exploration.

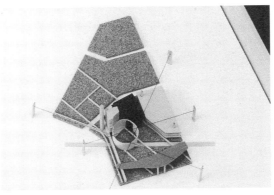

Diagram Model
A small model used to map out abstract site relationships and establish initial tectonic elements, such as the circular element.

Diagram Model
Three alternate spatial organizations diagram relationships between overall circulation and program issues.

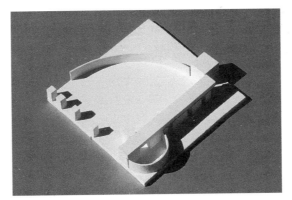

Diagram Model
Diagrams can be used to explore basic organizational schemes, such as a datum wall to set up overall relationships.

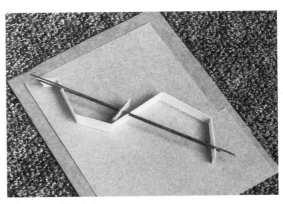

Diagram Model
Another simple diagram used to describe a contrasting relationship between the indirect processional element and the axial component.

Concept Models

Concept models are built at the initial stages of a project to explore abstract qualities such as materiality, site relationships, and interpretive themes. These models can be thought of as a specialized form of sketch models and are used as the "genetic coding" to inform architectural directions.

Translations can be made by a variety of means, such as dissecting the model with drawings, using suggested geometries, producing readings based on formal qualities, or interpreting literary themes.

The following concept models were established at the outset of several different projects. Although their use as genetic information is similar, their conceptual bases are quite different and illustrate the degree to which conceptual approaches can vary. Several other examples of concept models and architectural interpretations have been derived from these models. See "Interpreting" in Chapter 3.

Concept Model
A model made to explore ideas about shade, light, and shadow.

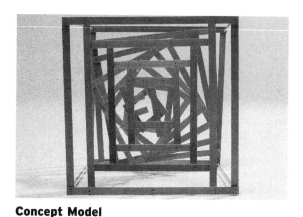

Concept Model
A model used to make interpretations of compartments and empty space, based on Andy Warhol's book *From A to B and Back Again.*

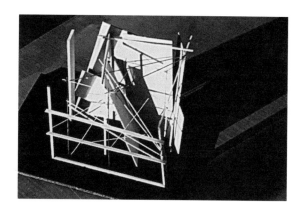

Concept Model
A model exploring abstract qualities of light and material relationships.

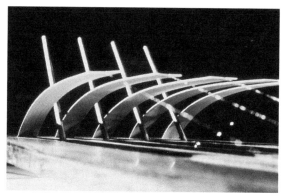

Concept Model
A spatial response to interpret passages from the book *Everglades: River of Grass,* by Marjory Douglas.

Massing Models

Massing models are simple models that depict volume and are typically devoid of openings. These models can be constructed at small scales because of their lack of detail and can quickly reflect a building's size and proportions at an early stage.

Massing models are used in a similar manner to sketch models and solid/void models. At times they may be built as partial solid/void models.

Massing Model
Small massing models are typical of the building representations used for site plans.

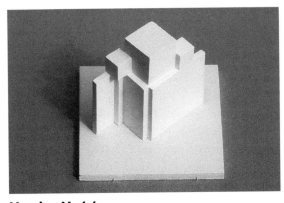

Massing Model
The kind of block massing typical of models that reflect only the solid form of the building.

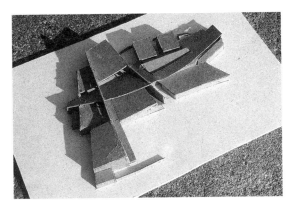

Massing Model
Very small models lend themselves to simple massing interpretations, as all but the largest voids will have little meaning at this scale.

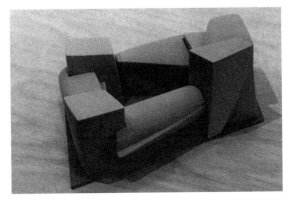

Massing Model
Massing models can be made in any number of forms, but their defining characteristic is the absence of openings.

Solid/Void Models

Solid/void models can be built as development or sketch models, but unlike massing models, they display the relationship between the open and closed areas of a building. Generally, these models are more useful for understanding a building's character than simple massing models. A comparison with massing models reveals the potential misreading of character conveyed by massing models, particularly in less conventional designs.

The examples primarily reflect models that have reached the stage of development models; however, any of these studies could have been made at a very small size and still have displayed the differences between open space and solid mass. The main difference imposed by size is that smaller openings can be omitted as the model is decreased in size.

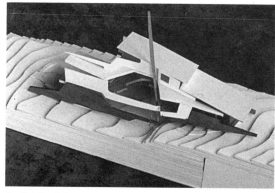

Solid/Void Model
The central void and linear nature of wall and roof planes is easily read in this solid/void study.

Solid/Void Model
This model type is somewhere between a development model and a refined sketch model *Note:* All major voids have been incorporated to reflect the light and open quality of the building.

Solid/Void Model
This model represents an extreme case in which the voids are all important and the use of pure massing would offer very little comprehension of the space.

Solid/Void Model
A simple model that can be visualized as a massing model, in comparison with the effect of cutting out primary openings.

Development Models

Use of development models implies that some initial decisions have been made and that a second or third level of exploration is being conducted. It also implies that the overall geometry remains fixed and at least one intermediate stage of exploration will be executed before the designer proceeds to the presentation model. This stage may involve looking at alternate wall treatments, refining proportions, or developing alternate elements.

Development models are typically increased in scale from the previous sketch studies to allow the designer to focus on the next level of design.

The examples can, in some instances, be considered finish models. The main difference is that they are essentially abstract representations of building relationships and are still open to modification and refinement. Moreover, they have not been detailed to reflect such aspects as material thickness and glazing.

In a number of cases, after further exploration, the building design may end with a development model, with drawing employed to communicate the final level of details.

For more on development models and their place in the progression of building design, see "Development" in Chapter 3.

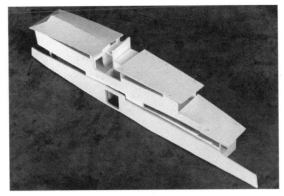

Development Model
After several studies, the model was built to reflect basic decisions accurately. At this stage relationships in the middle section of the building were refined, as well as wall and roof configurations.

Development Model
A typical level of design resolution at the development model stage. General building relationships have been established, but window openings and other details have been explored only in rough form.

Development Model
Complex geometric patterns have been established at this stage, but the model has not been taken to the level of defining glass planes and material hierarchies.

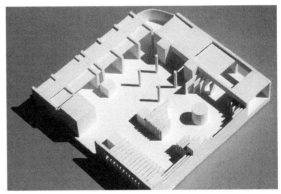

Development Model
This is a refined study model in which alignments have been carefully adjusted. At this stage the model is ready for the designer to begin applying architectural elements.

Presentation/Finish Models

The terms *presentation model* and *finish model* are used interchangeably to describe models that represent a completed design and are built with attention to craftsmanship.

They are used to confirm design decisions and communicate with clients who may not fully appreciate the implications of rougher studies.

Finish models are typically monochromatic constructions built from one material, such as foam core or museum board. This blank, abstract treatment allows the model to be read in many ways without the potential distractions of material simulations. White or light-colored materials such as balsa wood are also used, because they allow shadow lines, voids, and planes to be well articulated by light.

Finish Model
The abstract treatment of this model is typical of white, monochromatic finish models.

Finish Model
A simple finish model that employs two contrasting finishes to convey material qualities.

Finish Model Addition
The new building, made from lighter-colored balsa material is typical of monochromatic finish models. The existing buildings have been treated as darker elements to make the addition stand out.

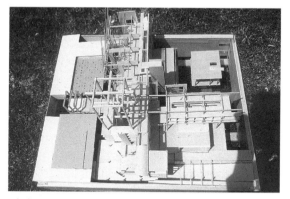

Finish Model
Even as an essential collection of lines, the monochromatic model treatment imparts an abstract reading, modeling forms in strong contrasting shadows.

Site Contour Models

Site models, or contour models, are built to study topography and a building's relationship to the site. They typically reproduce the slope of the land, or "grade," by employing a series of scaled layers that represent increments of rise and fall in the landscape.

As study constructions, they can be modified to fit the building to the site, control water, and implement landscape design.

Site Contour
A typical contour model displays site grades as regular intervals. Grade increments may represent anywhere from 6 in. to 5 ft, depending on the size of the site and the size of the model.

Site Contour
A steeply sloped site is modeled with faceted corrugated cardboard planes.

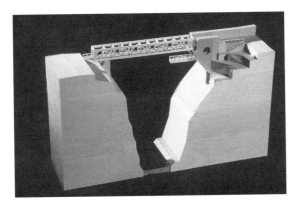

Site Contour
Steep site contours may be modeled as a section of property limited to the area of focus.

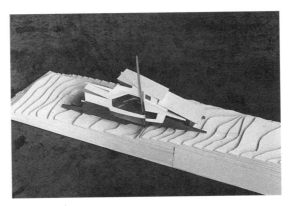

Site Contour
A site model is often limited to the property lines and appears as a section of the landscape.

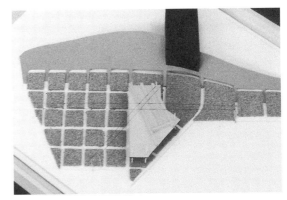

Site Contour
In modeling relatively large, flat areas such as urban blocks, contours may reflect only the gridded character of roads and streets.

Context Models

Context models are models that show the surrounding buildings. They are built to study a building's relationship to the mass and character of existing architecture. Context models can be used to show an existing building on the property or the neighboring area, or can be expanded to include an entire urban section.

Context models are incorporated into contour models and allow issues of grading and landscape design to be explored in relation to the building.

It is typical to treat the existing buildings of a context model as mass models, using neutral coloring to allow the new work to read as a contrasting construction.

Context models can be built to accommodate different projects by leaving a blank hole to fit various buildings into the site. In the example shown on the bottom right, the ground plane has been built over a hollow void. Context buildings are then inserted into the hole left in the surface material.

Site Context
This model uses an existing building (depicted in darker tones) as the site for a building addition. The building is needed for context and for scaling the addition.

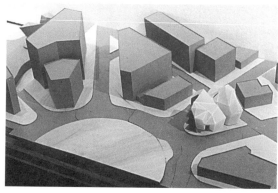

Site Context
The immediate context has been expanded to include buildings in a portion of an urban area. Although the buildings do not directly touch the site, they set the overall scale relationships between the existing and new.

Site Context
This model includes the immediate context buildings on an urban site. In this case, the scale and relationship between the existing building and the new structures are critical.

Site Context
At times, the context of an entire urban area is modeled as a means of accommodating alternate site selections and to understand the overall effect of the city.

Entourage/Site Foliage

Entourage refers to the modeling of people, trees, and site furnishings. Scaled figures are modeled, during the investigative stages, to give a sense of the scale of the building. Trees are included at the presentation stage (usually without people). Site furnishings, such as benches, lamps, and so forth, are typically reserved for more elaborate model simulations.

For design studies and finish models, it is best to treat foliage and entourage simply and abstractly. Elaborate simulations can easily overshadow a building both in terms of its psychological importance and by physically obscuring the project itself.

The examples offer several simple but effective methods used to provide unobtrusive site foliage. For more information on site foliage, see Chapter 2.

Entourage
Trees have been made by stacking layers of cut paper on wooden sticks. This method lends itself to larger-scale foliage.

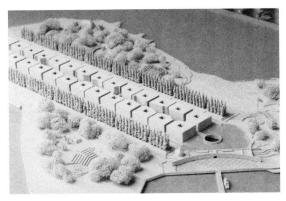

Entourage
Lichen and rolled paper trees have been used for small-scale foliage.

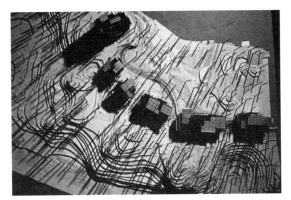

Entourage
Trees have been treated abstractly by using bare plastic rods. This gives a sense of wooded density without interfering with the perception of the building.

Entourage
Yarrow trees or dried plants can be used for larger-scaled models.

Interior Models

Interior models generally function as development models and are constructed to study interior architectural spaces and furnishings. They are built at scales starting at ¼″ = 1′-0″ but are more useful at ½″ = 1′-0″ and larger. These models should define the borders of the space but remain open for viewing and accessibility.

The design of interior spaces is approached much the same as the design of the building itself. A designer must realize that a building contains internal space worthy of the same consideration given to the exterior form. By opening up the building and "walking through" the space, observing it in three dimensions, many ideas can be generated.

Interior models typically employ various means to gain visual access to internal space. Rooftops can be removed to look down into the model, sides may be removed to gain horizontal access (as in section models), and holes can be cut into the underside to allow the viewer to look up into the space. In large models, very large openings in the bottom can permit total visual access.

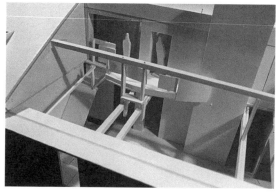

½ in. House Interiors Study
This ½″ = 1′-0″ scale foam core model employs a removable roof for viewing. The scale is large enough to permit reading of details as small as 1 in. and allows components to be developed inside the model.

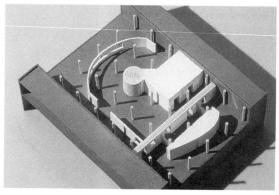

Interior Model
This is a case in which the entire design is an interiors project and the architecture is worked out in much the same way as external building design.

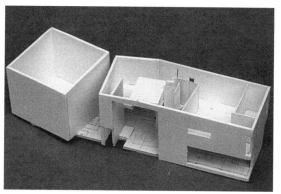

¼ in. House Interiors Study
Existing ¼″ = 1′-0″ scale models such as this are often large enough for the designer to develop interior partitions and circulation elements.

Interior Facade
In certain cases, elevations exist inside buildings. If a section is cut through the building to reveal internal elevations, interior and facade models become quite similar.

Section Models

Section models are built to study relationships between vertical spaces. They are produced by slicing the building at a revealing
location. The cut is usually made at the
point where a number of complex relationships interact, and can be jogged or sliced on
an angle if needed. The use of section models as study models can be most effective in
working out the complexities of relationships, which are often difficult to visualize
in two dimensions.

Section models are related to interior models in that they reveal interior spaces. One of
the key differences lies in their vertical ori-
entation, in contrast to the plan or top view
typically offered by interior models.

Section models are also closely related to
facade models and are sometimes referred to
as cutaway elevations or section/elevations.

Section Model
A section of a longer building reveals the play
of elements and spaces between floor plates,
balconies, and the roof form.

Section Model
This sketch model was built to explore relationships between internal floors and vertical
spaces. It can be thought of as an interior
model as well.

Section Elevation
A section taken through a column and arched
structure reveals space as a negative, carved
from solid material. This reading is in contrast
to the primarily voided sections in the other
examples.

Section Model
Section models can provide another way of
looking at interior spaces while maintaining
the relationships of the room in a way that
models with removed roofs cannot easily do.

Facade Models

Facade models are built when isolated elevations are needed for study and refinement. This situation typically occurs with infill buildings where the street elevation is the primary building image. In other cases, facades may be created to serve as context for additions to exterior elevations.

In the context of the urban street fabric, the manipulation of relatively shallow depths is used to create the illusion of greater spatial volumes. This can be taken further to look at the negative space produced by the facade and to generate new readings.

Although facade models are ideal study vehicles for flat, orthogonal elevations, they may not prove very useful in determining the character of nonorthogonal geometries.

As noted earlier, facade models and section/elevations can appear very similar to each other. Similarly, interior models can also include internal elevations.

Facade Model

A classic example of a facade as it might occur in an infill situation. Relatively flat elevations like this are well suited to facade model exploration.

Facade Model

The facade was built to serve as a background to develop the deck and entry canopies. *Note:* The windows have been drawn on, rather than cut out as in a solid/void study.

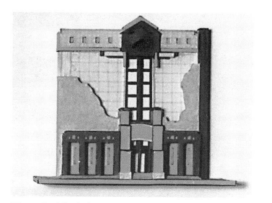

Facade Model

A facade model built to work out the design for an infill project.

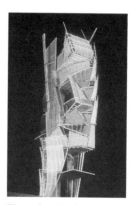

Facade Model

Although facade models are typically thought of as articulated flat elevations, isolated studies may also be conducted to focus on sculptural development of the exterior building face.

Framing/Structural Models

A framing/structural model is related to a detailing model in that its primary use is to help visualize the relationship between framing and structural systems in space. The exact location of beams, load transfers, and other technical considerations can then be determined. When built to large scales, framing models can be used to study the detailing of complex connections.

This model type can also be used to explore creative designs for structures such as bridges and trusses, to convey details to builders, and to test loading characteristics.

Framing models are built at relatively large scales (¼" = 1'-0" minimum) in order to show the relationship between members.

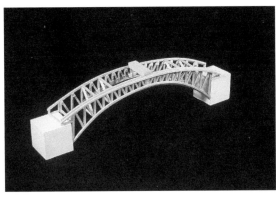

Framing Model
Framing models are used to work out the design and location of all structural members and can be extremely useful in working with complex geometries.

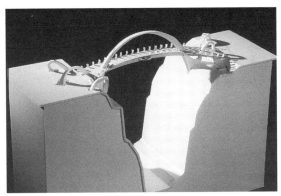

Structural Model
Models are useful in designing structural elements such as trusses and bridges. Not only do they allow visualization of the spatial concept, but member sizes can be refined to reflect structural and aesthetic concerns.

Structural Test
Large-scale models can be made to explore loading behavior. In this case a cardboard mockup has been loaded with bricks to test its capacity.

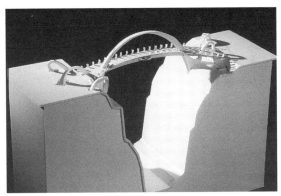

Bridge Model
The usefulness of a model in designing structural elements should be apparent when working out innovative solutions to architecturally designed structures such as this bridge.

Connection/Detail Models

Connection and detail models are built to develop interior and exterior details such as structural joints, window treatments, railings, and facias.

These models are treated in a similar manner as models of complete buildings but are built at much larger scales to allow finer readings of form articulation and connections.

Connection models are closely related to structural and framing models, as they provide a closer look at critical joints and intersections.

Scales typically range from ½" = 1'-0" to 3" = 1'-0". Detail models can be helpful in resolving design ideas and construction details, and in facilitating client communication.

The examples demonstrate various ways models can be used to develop building details or furnishings.

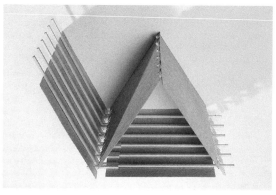

Connection Model
This study uses a model to explore the joint action and reading of members as they are folded together.

Building Detail Model
This window surround was built at 3" = 1'-0" (a relatively large scale) to study relationships between corner connections and wall depth. This is typical of the way models can be used to develop and refine building details.

Connection Model
This model has been built to focus on the design of a specific connection. The way the joint is expressed and its mechanical action have been worked out on the model.

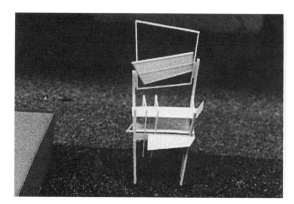

Furnishing Model
This small study for a movable book carrel was built to explore the effect of shades and adjustable racks.

CONNECT

Basic Techniques
for Assembling
Model Components

This chapter presents a catalog of basic modeling techniques. Many of the examples included here are presented throughout the book in the context of step-by-step models (see Chapter 4). This dual presentation is intended to convey an understanding of where and how the techniques may be used.

Cutting Materials

Cutting Sheets

Cutting sheet material, such as chipboard and foam core, is accomplished by applying light pressure on a knife and making multiple passes as required for material thickness. A sharp blade is needed, as well as a steel edge with nonslip backing or a steel-edged parallel bar. *Note:* Sheets should be cut on a cutting mat or other protective surface such as heavy cardboard.

Foam Core

Foam core is cut using multiple passes, similar to chipboard. Foam core will dull blades very quickly, and they must be changed often to avoid rough edges. The blade can be angled for mitered joints.

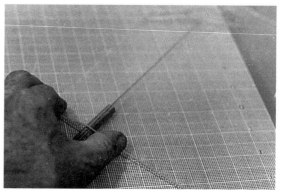

Plastic and Acetate

Plastic sheets are not cut through but must be scored with a sharp blade. This requires a little more pressure, and the score should be made in one accurate pass. After scoring, the score line should be placed over a hard edge, such as a knife handle, and broken by pushing down on both sides. To help cuts break cleanly, the raised edge may have to run continuously under the cut.

Paper and Cardboard

These materials are cut by pulling a knife in several passes, depending on thickness. A steel-edged parallel bar can be useful for making multiple components such as a series of parallel strips.

Balsa Wood Sheets

Balsa sheets can be treated similarly to heavy cardboard and foam core. Like foam core, balsa sheets are prone to rough edges if knife blades are not changed regularly.

Cutting Sticks and Wire

Sticks employed in model making are primarily made from wood, plastic, or wire. Most of these can be cut with a modeling knife, but for those that are large or harder, such as wire, saws and snips will be needed.

Plastic Sticks
Small rectangular sticks are cut in a similar manner to wood sticks. The ends can be squared with sandpaper.

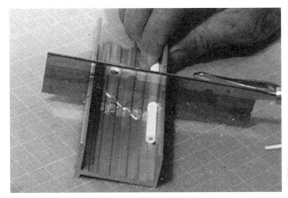

Large Wood and Plastic Sticks
For larger shapes, a modeling saw and miter box are needed. For difficult cuts, place the raised edge on the bottom of the box over a table edge and saw forward. Chipboard in the bottom of the box will protect the saw edge.

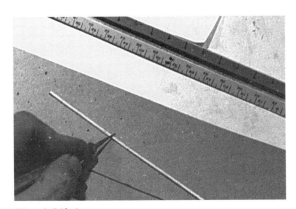

Wood Sticks
Small sticks can be cut by pressing down with a knife. Basswood sticks require more pressure and a slight sawing action. Rough edges can be squared with sandpaper. *Note:* Dull knife blades will crush the wood.

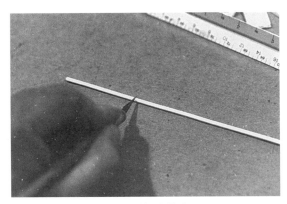

Round Wood and Plastic Sticks
Round sticks should be cut by rolling the knife. Small sticks can be cut completely through, but large ones should be scored and broken on the cut line. Rough ends can be dressed with sandpaper.

Wire and Metal Rods
Small wire snips can be used to cut rolls of copper and steel wire. Heavy electrical dikes are needed for harder rods. A small hacksaw and a miter box will be needed to saw bronze and copper tubes.

Cutting and Drilling Holes

There are a number of reasons for cutting holes in modeling sheets. Holes can serve as simple notches or sockets to receive other parts, they can provide a positive connection in the modeling base for a series of columns, or they can penetrate a number of common parts to create multiple floor plates.

Holes can be made by cutting or punching with a knife or by using a small electric drill. If a knife is used, a No. 11 blade, with its thin, tapered point, provides the best results.

Creating Sockets
Holes cut into the partial depth of foam core create a positive seat to insert columns. To excavate, insert a knife to the desired depth and rotate the blade. Make a tight fit, trying not to overcut the hole diameter.

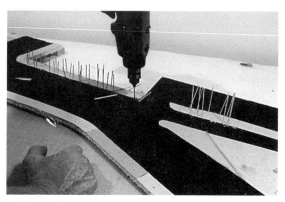

Drilling Column Holes
For speed and greater accuracy, an electric drill is useful. An added advantage is that holes can be excavated to greater depths without widening the entry point as a tapered knife blade tends to do.

Punching Column Lines
For quick studies, holes can be punched with a knife. The material will need some thickness, such as corrugated cardboard. Holes can almost be simple slits, into which the sticks are pushed.

Gang Drilling Holes
For multiple layers such as floor plates with column penetrations, the plates can be stacked, using pins to keep them aligned, and drilled through their the entire depth. *Note:* A base sheet is used to protect the cutting board.

Trimming and Clipping

In the course of model building it is often useful and necessary to make cuts directly on a model.

They can be used to make modifications to a study model, to refine a model, to fit parts, or to clean up connections.

Most trimming and clipping can be accomplished with a knife, a pair of scissors, and a small triangle.

Cutting New Openings

Openings can be cut with relative accuracy directly on the model, using a triangle as a guide and a very sharp knife. Rather than making several passes, push through the material and cut or saw in one pass.

Trimming and Modifying

Scissors can be effectively used on study models for quick cuts. They are less disruptive to lightly glued joints and are capable of making clean, straight cuts over small distances.

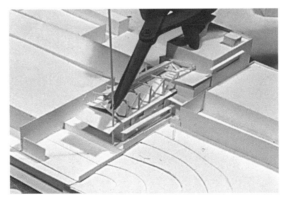

Trimming and Fitting

Small sticks can be trimmed in place with scissors, as their pincer action is less disruptive to delicate joints. This method also provides accuracy for fitting new parts to existing ones.

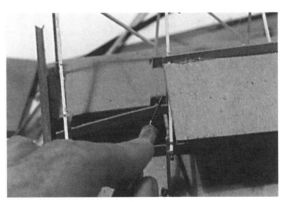

Cleaning Up Connections

Edges and other protrusions can be modified with a knife, by cutting or carefully shaving overlapping connections.

Attaching Parts

Attaching Planes

Model building for study purposes should be an ongoing process, with as little time as possible spent waiting for parts to dry. To this end, most materials are assembled with white glue.

When applied properly, white glue will dry quickly; however, cuts must be very straight for this method to work. In instances when drying time is not fast enough, a number of aids, such as the use of pins or tapes can be employed to allow the designer to continue working.

Assembling in Place
Glue can be applied to the material edge of assembled pieces directly on the model.

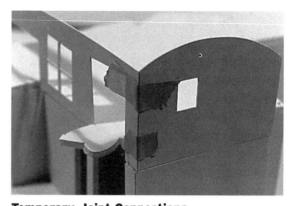

Temporary Joint Connections
For edges that do not dry immediately, use drafting tape for temporary connections. After 10 or 15 minutes, the tape can be removed. *Note:* Avoid masking tape and Scotch tape as they will tear paper surfaces.

Placing Glue
Keep glue in a pool to work from. This helps it to become thicker and can reduce drying time. Using a small cardboard stick, very lightly coat the edge of a material. Too much glue will cause joints to dry much more slowly.

Joining Parts
Press edges together and make sure that they are flush. After several seconds, the connection should be dry enough to hold on its own. Further drying will take place, but the part can be worked with right away.

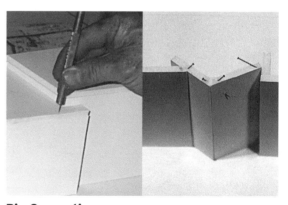

Pin Connections
Joints can be temporarily held together with straight pins, which are removed when glue is dry. In cases where joints will be hidden, pins can be pushed all the way in. The end of a knife handle is useful for setting and sinking pins.

It is important not to overglue study model components, as this tends to make them tear and deform when disassembled for experimentation.

Alternative Attachment Methods

There are several adhesives, other than white glue, appropriate to paper constructions, each with advantages and limitations. In applications where face gluing is encountered, such as in site models or paper coverings, the water content of white glue tends to buckle the paper. In these instances adhesives such as Spray Mount, hot glue, or double-faced tape are better choices.

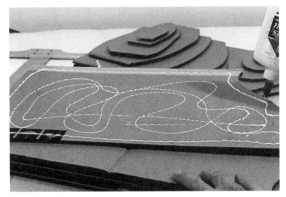

Face Gluing Contour Models
White glue is effective for thick materials such as corrugated cardboard. For site models that are to be experimented on, glue should be distributed in lines to allow alteration to the layers.

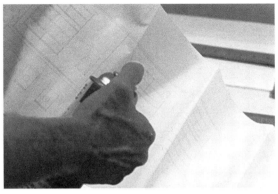

Nonbuckling Spray Adhesives
Apply a light, even coat of adhesive to attach cover materials and paper site contours. Site model contours can be modified as desired; however, holding power is limited.

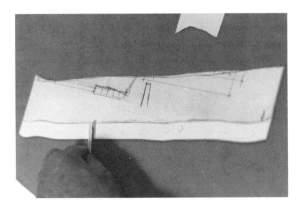

Face Gluing Sheets
White glue can be used on thick materials such as foam core and corrugated cardboard. For permanent, well-jointed connections, the glue should be spread evenly over the entire surface interface.

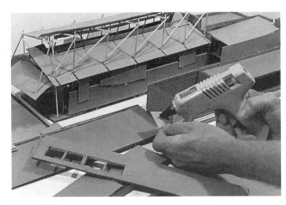

Hot Glue
Because of its quick setting time, hot glue is useful for quick sketch and study models where finished appearance is not demanding. Hot glue is also strong and can be used for reinforcing, but it tends to vibrate apart when moved.

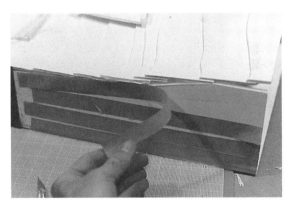

Covering with Transfer Tape
Fill in an area with strips, pull away the paper backing, and attach the cover sheet. Although this is an effective nonbuckling method, the cover sheet must be correctly aligned as there is no chance for further adjustment.

Integrating Forms

One of the key exercises in exploring readings between elements is to engage the parts in various relationships.

A rough study model makes this exercise quick and effective. Rather than avoiding difficult connections where model parts must share the same space, parts can be held in relative attitudes and quickly cut away, allowing the designer to visualize adjustments.

After final arrangements have been selected, the rough cuts can be recut or refaced (see "Converting" in Chapter 3).

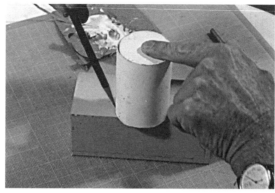

1. After building separate forms, the two parts are placed in approximate plan relationship and traced at the point of intersection. *Note:* For angled relationships, the plan locations of entry and exit can be of different sizes to reflect the diminishing penetration.

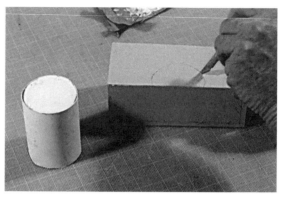

2. The point of penetration is cut out on the box top. *Note:* Material could have been removed from the cylinder instead of the box to achieve the intersection, but the cylinder would have been prone to come apart when this much material is removed.

3. Lines from the point of intersection are cut down the face of the box with the aid of a small triangle. *Note:* Blades must be sharp to do this without damaging the box. Scissors are sometimes better employed and create less disruption.

4. Material is removed from the box, and the parts are engaged by sliding the cylinder into the cut.

Attaching Sticks

Attachment methods appropriate to wood, plastic, and metal differ, depending on the material and the level of finish desired.

Wood sticks typically use white glue. Hot glue can be used in applications where greater speed is desired.

Plastic sticks are attached with specially designed acetate adhesive, although model airplane glue can be used with some success. It is possible to glue plastic sticks with hot glue for quick studies, but the plastic surface can reject the glue. When attaching plastic sticks to paper, white glue or hot glue must be used in place of the acetate.

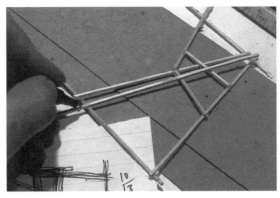

Wood Sticks
Apply a touch of white or hot glue to end connections and joints. To keep glue from sticking to working surfaces, place the construction on top of plastic food wrap or another nonstick surface.

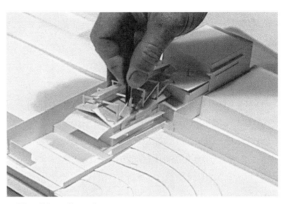

Attaching in Place
Apply a drop of acetate to the end of a stick and place it in contact with the existing framework. Light sticks can be released within a few seconds and allowed to remain in place to dry.

Plastic Sticks
Place a drop of acetate on the end of a knife blade and transfer it to the joint. The material should be ready to use in less than a minute.

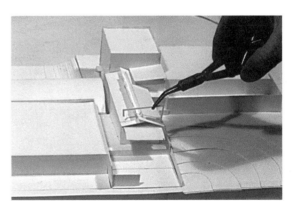

Attaching Dissimilar Materials
Plastic components must be interfaced with paper using white glue, as acetate adhesive will not work with paper or cardboard.

Attaching Plastic Sheets and Wire

Relatively standard methods using acetate adhesive are employed for plastic sheet connections and offer predictable results.

Wire and metal connections in model applications present several problems, and no one solution is ideal. Because white glue does not adhere well to metal, the most practical and effective alternatives are hot glue, super glue, and solder. Of these, only hot glue will interface with paper with relative success. Even then, results are mixed and a combination of drilled sockets and white glue may be necessary to achieve the desired connection.

Attaching Plastic Sheets
Spread a thin line of acetate adhesive along the edge of the material. *Note:* A third hand is provided by the needle nose pliers.

Attaching Wire and Metal
Hot glue can be used; however, joints will not hold if rotated. The use of super glue and delicate handling is another alternative. White glue can hold to a degree, but must be dried for several hours.

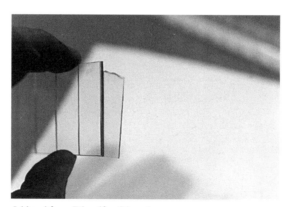

Attaching Plastic Sheets
After applying the acetate adhesive hold the edges together and wait a minute or more before testing. Joints will be fragile and attaching them can be time-consuming. *Note:* Cuts must be straight or it will be difficult for the glue to adhere.

Acid Core-Solder Connections
Heat the wire with a soldering gun near the connection point. Test the wire temperature with the end of the solder. When the solder melts, apply it to the connection point and allow it to cool. Do not melt solder directly with the soldering gun.

Fitting Components
Aligning Edges

Once a model is partially constructed, irregularities such as minor misalignments, offsets because of material thickness, and stretched blueline drawings are inevitable despite attention to accuracy. To help ensure tight connections, model components cut from plan and elevation drawings should be checked with the emerging model dimensions before assuming that blueline templates will produce parts that fit.

To keep component edges plumb and square, a small triangle can be used. A triangle is particularly important for vertical alignment inasmuch as no drawing lines will be available to follow.

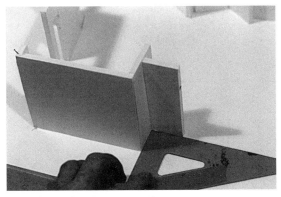

Aligning Plan Components
Place a small triangle at wall intersections and align the parts with triangle edges. For angled intersections, use an adjustable triangle. If walls are short, template the angle off the triangle, cut out the shape, and use it to align the model parts.

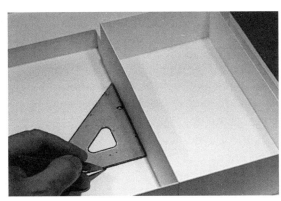

Drafting on the Model
Small triangles can be used to draft guidelines on the model. This is useful when a model is being made without drawings or when new components are added.

Vertical Alignment
For vertical alignment, hold the part directly against the triangle, or mark guidelines on the adjoining wall face.

Detailing Connections

As models become larger and more refined, joints reflect greater levels of detail. Edges should read clearly and be accurately scaled. Thicker materials should be dovetailed to conceal interior layers, particularly with the use of colored boards with nonintegral interior layers.

Several conventions are used to code building parts. One of the most commonly employed is the use of standing edges to simulate parapet walls at the perimeter of low-slope roofs.

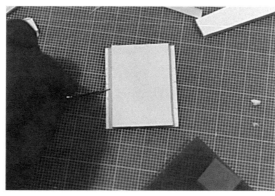

90 Degree Foam Core Intersections
Cut a line into the foam filler equal to the thickness of the intersecting wall and scrape away all the foam down to the paper backing. The remaining paper face can then fit neatly over the edges of intersecting walls.

Corner Detailing
Another method of achieving tight-fitting corners is to cut the material on an angle as shown. The cuts must be accurate for a good fit, but the angle can vary on the tight side if only one side is exposed.

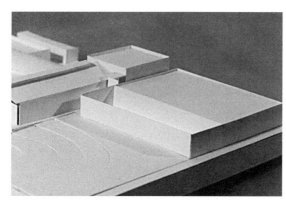

Roof Detailing Conventions
The plane of the low-slope roofs on this context model have been set slightly below the perimeter walls to create a parapet wall. This convention helps code the roof plane as being visually different from the ground plane.

90 Degree Intersection
The wall is placed next to its adjoining parts. As the wall is fitted together, the edges will meet without any of the core material being revealed.

Compound Joint Detailing
Joints that angle in more than one direction, or "compound joints" such as shown in the upper right corner of the illustration, can be made by cutting and adjusting test fits, then templating the two ends onto a single piece the full width of the opening.

Handling Small Parts

As model parts become more delicate and refined, it may not be possible to place them by hand. A few simple tools can be employed to make clean connections.

In the illustrations to the right, tweezers, needle nose pliers, and a modeling knife are used in various applications. Although their uses can overlap, certain tools are better suited to particular situations than others.

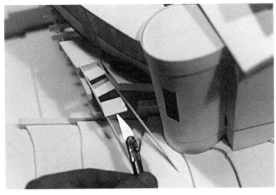

Knife Edge Placement
By inserting the tip of the modeling knife into the paper edge, components can be guided into place. Care must be taken to lightly engage the knife or parts can be pulled free when extracting the blade.

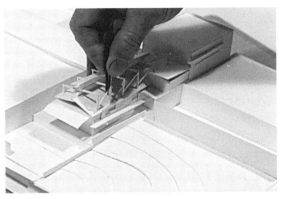

Tweezers for Delicate Members
The automatic-release spring action of tweezers allows placement without disturbance, and they can handle parts, such as plastic, that a knife cannot easily penetrate.

Knife Face Placement
Parts can be placed with a knife by gently inserting the knife in the face of the material. Too much blade engagement may leave visible marks in the surface.

Plier Grips
Although it is not as easy to release objects from pliers as from tweezers, needle nose pliers offer a steady grip for positive placement. By keeping one finger inside the handle, they can be gently opened to release components.

Shaping and Reinforcing

Making curvalinear shapes from various materials can be accomplished in a number of ways. Many specialized techniques are covered in Chapter 5; however, two very common techniques for curving and warping planes are useful at even the basic levels of model building. Planes can be rolled or applied to a series of curved frames.

After pieces have been curved, they can be cut along bias lines to form a number of derivative shapes. Planes can also be made to fit curved armatures and warped in an infinite variety of ways.

For larger components, holding an accurate radius on a curved piece requires some type of reinforcing members. These can usually be hidden inside wall lines or disguised in some way, as they are not really parts of the building. This is not to say that they may not become part of the building, because these components may generate ideas for holding the actual building radii and be incorporated into the design.

Reinforcements are also useful under long spans of thin board and at wall edges to support planes and roofs inserted into perimeter walls.

Roof Ledger
A ledger strip has been attached to the wall slightly below the top so that the roof can be dropped in and carried on an even line. The cardboard stick is being used to press the strip against the wall until it sets.

Curving Cardboard
Board can be curved by rolling it over cylindrical objects. It can be pulled across small cylinders for a tight radius or molded on larger objects for gentler curves. Forms should be slightly over-rolled, then relaxed to fit.

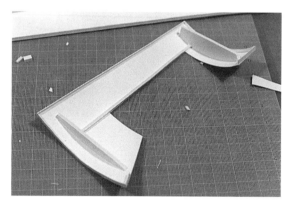

Reinforcing Curves
To maintain large radiuses, curved reinforcing sections of foam core have been glued into place. Note the edge fascia detailing using scaled curved pieces.

Warped Surfaces
Thin plastic mylar sheets and tracing paper can be glued to wire or cardboard frames and made to conform to various compound curves. Mylar tends to simulate the qualities of glass but is less pliable than paper.

Templating

Transferring Drawings

One of the quickest methods for transferring drawn information to modeling components is to template them. This is done by cutting through the drawings to score the material below. The drawing is then removed and parts are attached, using the score lines as a layout guide.

Alternately, the plans can remain mounted to the model surface and built directly on top of it. Aside from the visual distraction, this sometimes causes problems, as the walls are glued to the drawing and the drawing is attached only with spray adhesive.

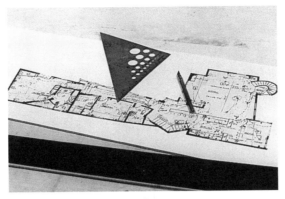

Plan Readied for Transfer

In a typical transfer operation, the plan is secured to the modeling sheet with spray adhesive, then traced lightly with a knife using steel drafting edges. The plan is then removed, and the lightly cut lines are followed when placing components.

Cutting in Elevations

The drawing is cut all the way through to create the fenestration pattern. To avoid overcutting the corners, either finish the cuts from the opposite side or penetrate the knife through the board and saw at a 90 degree angle. *Note:* Only the larger window mullions have been reproduced. See "Scale" in Chapter 3.

Spray Adhesive

Apply a light, even coat of adhesive in a well-ventilated area, then spread out the plan smoothly on the material surface by attaching the corners and smoothing it down from one end. For large plans, a third hand may be needed.

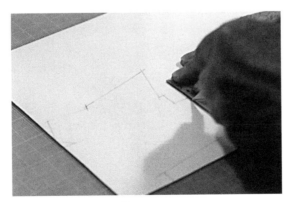

Drafting with a Knife

Even without plans, a layout can be drafted onto the modeling material with a knife, just as one might draft on paper with a pencil.

Templating Parts

Parts can be templated, that is, traced directly from the outline of another component, or measured directly from drawings without the use of a ruler.

For complex connections, the process may have to be repeated several times while adjusting the new part each time to fit into the desired form.

Typical Templating Application
A form can be cut to the model shape by tracing around the form and cutting out the desired piece. In the illustration, a top for an irregularly curved conical tower is quickly made using this method.

Templating Contours
In a manner similar to projecting contour lines in a section drawing, a side cover is made by placing the modeling material next to the existing model contours and tracing the profile.

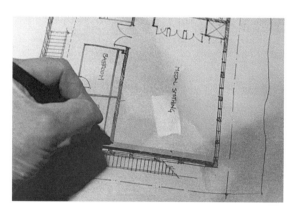

Measuring from Drawings
As the model proceeds, parts such as ledgers and other components can be marked directly from the drawings.

Templating Complex Forms
For complex forms, a rough version can be cut or approximated from several spliced pieces, then transferred to another sheet with adjustments. This can be done several times until the final piece fits accurately.

Projecting Lines
Accurate cuts on the model may be located by extending a line with a straightedge to find the intersection point with another component.

Templating Multiples

A template can also be a device that is used repeatedly to reproduce a single item. Templates can be made and used for model building. A very practical application is using a template to make a series of repetitive roof trusses.

This technique can employ a range of approaches, from drawing a simple template to building a model jig for mass assembly.

Drawn Template

A simple template can be made by tracing the design on paper and laying each new component over the drawing.

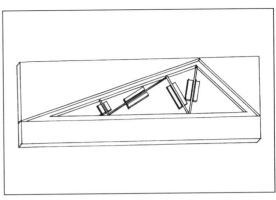

Block-Type Jig Template

Pin-type jigs can be improved by cutting blocks and gluing them to a base to form the boundary edges for truss members. Block-type jigs are stronger and may be needed when making curved trusses.

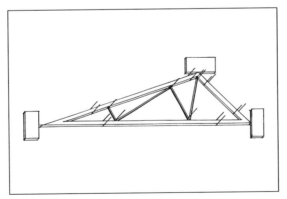

Pin-Type Jig Template

Pin templates can be made by inserting straight wire pins in a base and laying members inside the defining points.

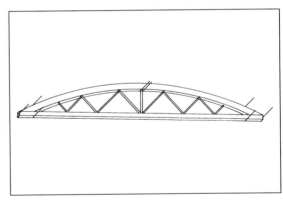

Braced Curve Template

Curved members can be made by pinning the two ends and using restraining pins in the middle. Once web members are installed and end connections are made sound, the truss should hold its shape without the pins.

Finishes

Fenestration

Fenestration, or the act of creating windows and glazed openings, can be accomplished in a variety of ways.

Guidelines for denoting openings are to keep them simple and to detail only what can be accurately depicted at scale. *Note:* It is usually better to avoid drawing openings on surfaces.

For alternate glazing simulations, overlays can be used, as well as plastic sheets with applied mullion patterns.

Fenestration Overlay
A simple overlay can be cut and placed on top of a base sheet to provide a subtle reading of openings.

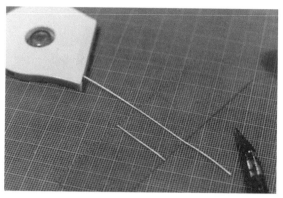

Art Tape on Plastic Sheet
Art tape can be stretched across plastic to create mullions, using score lines as guides. Trim the tape ends after they have been pressed down.

Curtain Wall Glazing
Even small models can use plastic glazing sheets to create glass walls. For small areas and curved pieces, thick acetate can be used. As size increases, sheets of thin plastic will be needed to maintain rigidity.

Scoring Mullion Lines
Lines can be scored in plastic with a knife to serve as the actual mullion pattern or as guidelines for applying art tape.

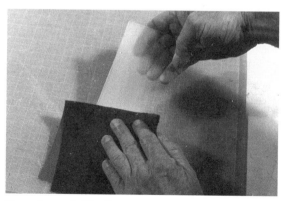

Translucent Glazing
Translucent glass can be made from plastic or thin Plexiglas sheets by sanding one side with very fine paper.

Surfacing

For simple presentation models, final detailing and finishing can be accomplished through clean construction and a few simple techniques.

Surfaces can be covered with additional layers of paper board to clean up exposed joints and create opening patterns. Edges can be detailed to convey correctly scaled depths.

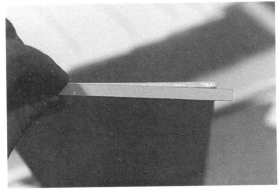

Edging Detailing

Museum board strips, cut to the exact scale of the desired fascia details, are adhered to the edge of ⅛ in. foam core roof panels. The factory edges of foam core and cardboard sheets are commonly too thin to convey the correct reading for ¼ in. scale.

Painting

Models can be cleaned up and finished by light spray painting. Flat automotive primer is recommended as an undercoat for heavy spray painting to prevent the paper from buckling.

Covering

The model is in the process of being covered with colored construction paper. This is applied by coating the paper with spray adhesive, but there is a limited time before it separates from the model. For more permanent applications, transfer tape should be used.

Sanding

Rods and sticks can be sanded by rubbing them back and forth across a sheet of sandpaper placed on a flat surface; 100 grit paper will serve for most purposes.

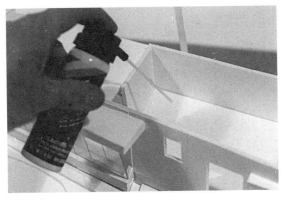

Cleaning

Models littered with postconstruction debris can benefit from cleaning with blasts of compressed air.

Site Work
Solid Contour Model

Select a material thickness that will scale to the desired grade steps. In the example, the scale is ⅛" = 1'-0", and the corrugated cardboard is ⅛ in. thick, representing 1 ft grade steps.

Adhesive Guide

Spray Mount (Spay-Type Adhesives)

Thin chipboard and paper models work best with spray adhesives, inasmuch as the water in white glue tends to buckle the material. Foam core can work with either spray adhesive or white glue. For study models, spray-mounted model layers are much easier to modify.

White Glue

For heavy materials such as corrugated cardboard, white glue may be needed for strength. It can be spread evenly for permanent construction, or applied in lines to allow for removal of the layers. White glue can take up to 12 hours to dry when applied to the face of a material.

Hot Glue

Hot glue can be used but can be difficult to disassemble for modifications. Moreover, as the model is moved around, hot glue tends to lose its grip.

1. Use a copy of the contour map to template the cuts (apply with spray adhesive to keep it from shifting). The copy can be cut to score the surface of the cardboard, or a pizza cutter can be rolled over the lines to transfer marks to the material.

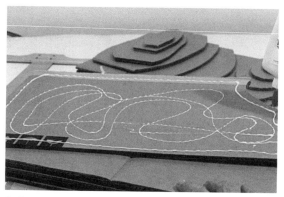

2. Starting with a full sheet the size of the site, cut away the first contour line. Glue this sheet to a base sheet the size of the entire site.

3. Cut away the next contour from another full sheet, and place this one on top of the first contour. All layers can be stacked first without gluing. When prestacking layers, splice lines should be marked and grades labeled to help guide reassembly.

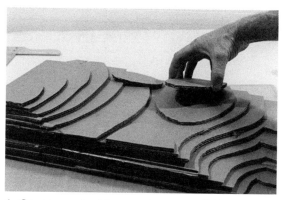

4. Continue stacking contours until they are small enough to use partial sheets, as for hilltops and other small sections. Grades can be lightly labeled on each contour to aid in counting elevations and controlling site work.

Drying

After gluing, the model is weighed down with books or magazines to press layers tight until they are set.

Hollow Contour Model

Hollow models are built in a similar manner to solid ones, but only partial sheets are needed.

Contours can be either cut away to insert building volumes or built up around buildings. *Note:* Be careful not to cut along each contour without providing extra material for overlap between the sheets.

See Chapter 4, "Case Study A," for an example built directly on the model.

1. Cut sheets with enough area behind the contour lines to allow an adequate gluing surface (about ½ in. to 1½ in., depending on the size of the exposed piece and the weight of the material). Mark the edges to keep glue out of areas that will be exposed.

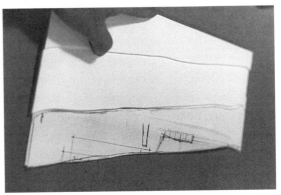

2. Splice the successive contour layers to each other and provide support from below to hold the construction at the proper slope. This can be done by building a series of columns or templating a section with graded steps that follow the rise of each contour.

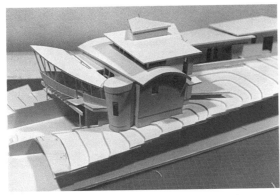

3. With most of the contours in place, the cavity below is clearly evident, as well as the overlapping splices between partial pieces.

4. Small grade sections can be completed off to the side and installed as a unit.

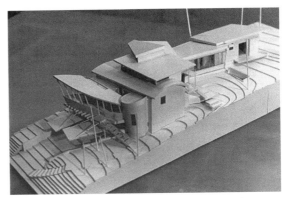

5. The finished construction has side walls added to support the edges at the proper rate of rise. To cut support walls, lay the model on its side and template the pieces. Side pieces can also be drafted as a section projection of the contour map.

Site Foliage

For design studies and simple finish models, it is best to treat foliage and entourage simply and abstractly. Elaborate simulations can easily overshadow a building, both in terms of its psychological importance and in the way they visually obscure the project.

Illustration

The examples offer simple but effective methods commonly used to provide unobtrusive site foliage.

The images at bottom right corner are larger illustrations of the materials used for trees.

Foliage A

Trees have been created using lichen placed on small sticks. The lichen does not interfere with the ability to see the project and works well at small scales.

Foliage B

Trees have been made by stacking layers of cut paper on wooden sticks. This method works better for larger-scale foliage.

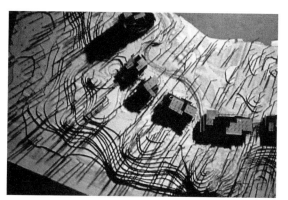

Foliage C

The trees have been treated very abstractly by using bare plastic rods to give a sense of wooded density without interfering with the visibility of the building.

(*a*) Small dried flowering plants or yarrow trees; (*b*) lichen, sold as modeling material or found in sandy areas.

(*c*) Paper and Styrofoam layers; (*d*) wood or plastic dowels.

Model Base Construction

A number of bases are shown throughout the chapters of this book, and the discussion on contour models in Chapter 2 provides the basic information for base construction. However, some general guidelines can are given here.

The main objective of a base is to support the model without warping or sagging. This is easily accomplished with small models but requires reinforcement and heavier material as models gain weight and size. Deep reinforced bases, Gatorboard, and plywood offer solutions in such cases.

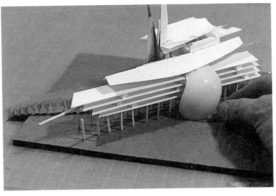

Sketch Model Base

Small sketch models can be built on pieces of corrugated cardboard or foam core. Layers can be stacked in rough simulations of sloped sites.

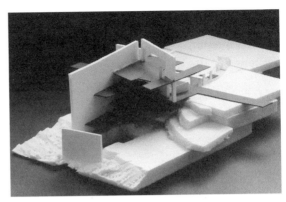

Study Model Base

Foam can be used to create quick grade simulations and provide instant rigidity.

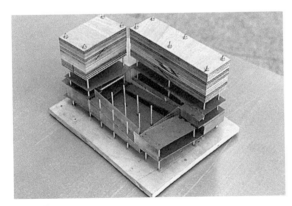

Flat Base

For heavy models such as this solid wood construction, plywood or Gatorboard can be used to make flat bases.

Reinforced Bases

For large models with flat bases, boxes with top and bottom surfaces can be built and reinforced with a internal strips running at 90 degrees inside the box. Increasing the box depth will add strength.

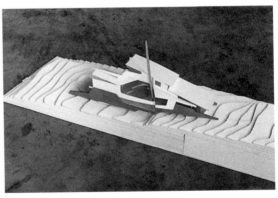

Hollow Contour Bases

Although solid contour models tend to become rigid of their own accord, it is often necessary to reinforce the internal spaces of hollow bases with cardboard uprights and horizontal strips.

EXPLORE

A Skeletal Framework for Conceiving and Using Models

The design process is an evolutionary event that involves establishing a direction and developing it through experimentation and refinement. At each stage, a range of studies should be conducted to explore the direction and strength of various design moves.

An Overview of Section Concepts

The following outline presents an overview of the typical stages in the design process for models. The considerations are similar to those for drawn projects, but most of the required information is derived directly from the model. *Note:* The linear form of the outline is one of convention, as many of the steps may be combined or used interactively.

SCALE

Determining appropriate scale based on:

Project Size
Fitting the building and site to the available work space

Type of Study
Adjusting for the stage of development

Level of Detail
Scaling for the size of details being explored

Assigned Scale
Determining scale, after making concept and sketch models without using a fixed scale

IDEAS

Generating initial information through:

Drawing with the Model
Sketching ideas exclusively with the model, using expressive and carefully proportioned approaches

Working with Two-Dimensional Drawings
Working back and forth between drawn and modeled information

ALTERNATIVES

Exploring design directions by:

Multiple Approaches
Building multiple solutions or testing multiple treatments on a single model

Adjustable Models
Using movable parts to explore alternative relationships

SITE

Integrating site concerns with other design information:

Contour Models
Including site information as an integral part of the initial driving forces for design direction

Context Models
Responding to environment as it affects initial design direction

MANIPULATION

Working with models to visualize options:

Modifying and Editing
Cutting and adding parts to design directly on the model

Modifying Site Contours
Integrating the building with the site

Digression
Using the unexpected to inform and maintain design ideas

Interpreting
Making a fundamental shift in the physical form or perception of the model

DEVELOPMENT

Developing the project by:

Project Development
Exploring an evolutionary path from initial concepts to a complete project

Increasing Scale
Building larger models as the investigation moves from general concerns of site and scheme to focused concerns of elevations, interior space, and detailing

Coding and Hierarchy
Establishing hierarchy and coding to define a range of contrasting elements and code conceptual layers

Converting
Renovation of existing models versus entirely rebuilding

Focusing
Moving studies through successive stages of refinement

Scale

Key Scaling Issues

Models can be built at various scales. The size of the model may not be indicative of the scale, as physically large models may be built at small scales and vice versa.

Determining the appropriate scale depends on several considerations, as discussed in the following paragraphs.

Project Size

The size of the model depends on how large the actual building and or site will be and is governed by the availability of work space.

Type of Study

The scale and size of the model depend on the type of study that is being conducted, such as sketch, development, presentation, interior, or detail.

Level of Detail

The scale of the model depends on the level of detail that is needed. A prime reason to increase a model's scale is to include more detail. A scaled-up model without additional detail may appear ungainly. Accordingly, it can be more convincing and practical to imagine fine details on smaller models than to construct large models with insufficient detail.

Assigned Scale

By maintaining the relative proportion between components, models may be initiated without using a particular scale. A scale can then be assigned to a model after it is built. This technique is useful in small sketch studies.

In this case, a small model of a human figure can be made to a size that is correctly proportioned to the building model in relation to how the designer envisions the actual size of the building. The "full scale"

height of the figure (assumed to be approximately 6 ft), can then be compared to various scales on a scale ruler to find the one that matches the 6-ft dimension of the model figure. This scale can then be assigned to the building model and used to determine its actual, "full scale" dimensions. This can also be done by assuming a typical floor to floor height of 12–14 ft on a multistory building (or as appropriate to the project such as 9–11 ft for a typical residential model). The designer then can compare various scales on the ruler to find the one that matches the floor to floor heights on the model at the assumed "full scale" dimension. For small models it will probably be necessary to use an engineering scale rule, where scales between 1″ = 20′ and 1″ = 200′ are available. For an example of this technique at work see Chapter 4, "Case Study B."

EXAMPLES: SCALE DECISIONS
AND CONSIDERATIONS

- A typical model of a house may be scaled at a maximum of ¼″ = 1′-0″, so that an actual length of 96 ft would occupy 2 ft of desk space or work area where the designer is to build the model.

- For a larger building involving several hundred feet, a scale of ⅛″ = 1′-0″ may be used effectively.

- Large sites usually use engineering scales of 1″ = 50′, 100′, or 200′ to make the model manageable.

- Sketch models typically start at very small scales, such as ¹⁄₃₂″, ¹⁄₁₆″, or ⅛″ = 1′-0″, and focus on general relationships. As the design direction is further developed, models can be increased in scale to study detailed issues.

- Models needed for context only may be scaled at smaller sizes, such as 1″ = 20′ or ¹⁄₁₆″ = 1′-0″.

- Presentation models are generally effective if they are built large enough to be detailed. For a house, the scale could be ¼″ = 1′-0″ or larger. For a large building, ⅛″ = 1′-0″ may be an appropriate size.

- Modeling details must be constructed to scale. This consideration makes it very difficult to simulate dimensions such as 2 or 3 in. at a scale of ⅛″ = 1′-0″ or smaller.

- For studies such as window mullions, roof facia, and connections, larger scales such as ½″ or 1″ = 1′-0″ are needed.

- For smaller scales, fine details should be implied.

Ideas

Expressive Model Drawing

Strategy

Models assembled with the speed of two-dimensional sketching can be effectively used as the prime generators of information without the aid of drawings or exact scales. To facilitate this, begin by becoming very familiar with the basic program, site conditions, and structural options until they become part of the designers internal knowledge of the project parameters. These can then be put aside to approach the model from another perspective. It may be difficult at first to reconcile practical concerns with your discoveries; however, with experience, they can be intuitively approximated and later used to inform design moves.

Although the model need not be built to a predetermined scale, it should employ relatively proportioned relationships between its parts, such as floor-to-floor heights. These heights can be measured later and assigned a scale to fit the project. For more information on assigning scale, see "Scale" earlier in this chapter and "Case Study B" in Chapter 4.

Illustration

Abridged steps are shown from the beginning phases of two different projects. Although specific project requirements were in mind, sketch models were constructed without exact scales or drawings to generate initial ideas.

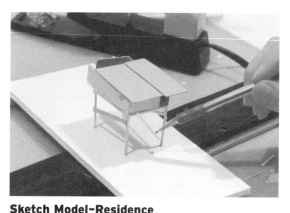

Sketch Model-Residence
A small frame is erected and used to visualize successive moves.

Sketch Model-Office Building
Columns are installed, and a stack of floor plates are mounted on top. *Note:* Floor plates have been separated by small pieces of foam core to establish equal floor-to-floor heights.

Sketch Model-Residence
The basic form is established, and pieces are added as they contribute to the expression of the model.

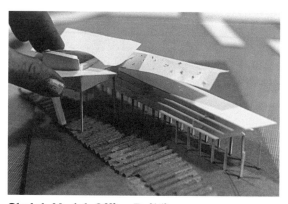

Sketch Model-Office Building
The unit is tested for design fit by holding it up to various locations on the framework until an optimum relationship is determined.

Additive/Subtractive Drawing

Strategy

One way of approaching three-dimensional forms is in terms of additive and subtractive operations. In additive operations individual components are joined together to form a construction. In subtractive operations, models are initiated with a block of material and pieces are subtracted to arrive at the design. Additive processes are more often associated with solid/void models, and subtractive models and mass models are closer in conception. In practice, a combination of additive and subtractive approaches are employed.

Illustration

The two projects on the immediate right use additive and subtractive processes, respectively.

Formal Proportioning

Strategy

Another important approach is to use the model as a device for refining proportion and making exacting spatial alignments. This approach requires tighter control and greater attention to crafting the model, and focuses on placement and adjustment as its primary concerns.

Illustration

The example on the far right illustrates space developed through careful alignment of forms and proportion.

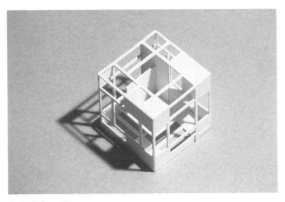

Additive Space
Individual planes and sticks have been joined together in an additive process to define a space. The reverse perception of the cube might see it as a solid, carved away to leave the voids.

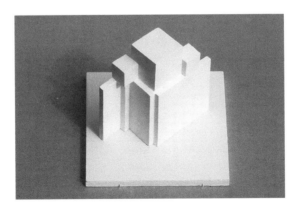

Subtractive Space
The massing model can be perceived as having been carved away from a solid block. Although typically thought of as a subtractive procedure, the reverse perception might see the model as an additive construction.

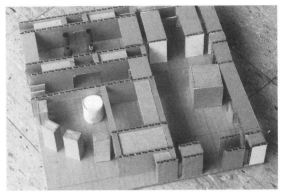

Alignment Sketch Model
The model is used as a drawing tool in this instance to develop controlled relationships between elements. Although its focus is more rational, it serves as a sketch model similar to those used for other types of approaches.

Alignment Development Model
Modeling precision is increased as the study is refined. The idea of drawing as an exercise in fine-tuning proportion and alignment becomes well defined with this model.

Working with Plan and Elevation Drawings

Strategy

The sketch model can be used in concert with simple scaled drawings to set a general direction. Once the building begins to emerge, the model can be used as a focal point to help visualize additional design decisions. Conversely, design elements carried out on the model can be used to refine drawings such as elevation studies, which in turn can be used to inform the model. The key to using each effectively is to decide which medium offers more efficiency and at the same time provides useful information in relation to the investigation at hand. For example, at the development stage, elevation drawings of flat walls can be more effective in refining compositions than a model. Conversely, elevations of a sculptural building geometry may offer little useful information about the building, as compared with a model. This type of dialogue between drawn information and modeled information can be one of the most efficient means for project development.

Illustration

The projects to the right were initially generated from scaled schematic plans and sketches.

Schematic Drawings

Relatively large-scaled drawings (⅛″ = 1′-0″) were used to establish this development model. In this instance, there was no sketch model, as the orthogonal geometries were worked out in 2-D drawings. A large model was needed to develop the external frame and wall details. *Note:* Model parts were cut directly from the drawings. For a step-by-step illustration of the model assembly, see Case Study C in Chapter 4.

Schematic Drawings

Small-scaled plan and section studies were used to produce the initial model information. Curved pieces are measured directly from the actual model radiuses. *Note:* For a step-by-step illustration of the model assembly. see Case Study D in Chapter 4.

Working with Concept Drawings

Strategy

Another way of approaching the relationship between two-dimensional drawings and three-dimensional constructions is to exploit the conceptual dialogue between the two mediums. In this process, drawings such as collages and paintings can be interpreted to produce three-dimensional forms and, conversely, models can be interpreted as drawings to set up orthogonal plan and section relationships.

This process is usually carried out in the early stages of a project, and constructions typically require further interpretation to move them forward into architectural propositions.

Once the basic operation is understood, this relationship can be transferred back and forth a number of times to develop an evolving process. For related examples, see "Interpreting" later in this chapter.

Illustration

The following five projects show examples of drawing and model strategies used to work with drawings in this way. In the first three projects the model preceded the drawing and was interpreted to generate it. In the last two projects, the two-dimensional drawing was interpreted to generate the three-dimensional forms.

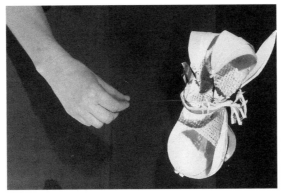

Project 1 Pattern Model

The model was developed using pattern pieces, through the process described in Manipulation Patterning Interpreting-Pattern.

Project 2 Transformer Model

This model explored the idea of change and transformation. The potential unfolding of its components was analyzed in the accompanying drawings.

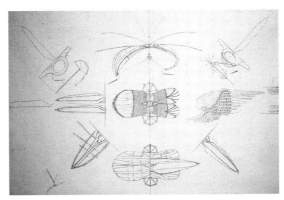

Project 1 Pattern Drawing

The object was carefully dissected with elevation and section drawing studies and reduced to a set of two-dimensional diagrams.

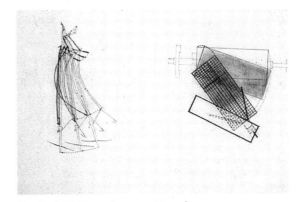

Project 2 Transformer Drawing

Drawings of the model in motion were subsequently used as abstract generative information to begin plan and section studies.

Project 3 Precedence
The model was built in response to the space of a precedent model with a process similar to that described in "Manipulation/Interpreting-Precedent Interpretation" in this chapter.

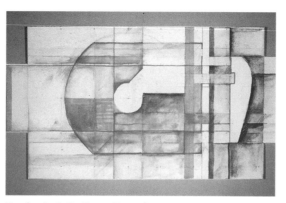

Project 4 Collage Drawing
The collage was designed as an abstract composition from a series of overlays. Once experience is gained with the process, elements can be controlled to help facilitate specific program needs.

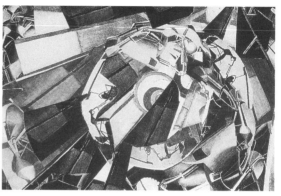

Project 5 Duchamp Collage Drawing
A collage drawing created from Marcel Duchamp's *Nude Descending a Staircase* served as the initial design move.

Project 3 Drawing of Model Space
The model was used as a site to interpret qualities of light and spatial experience.

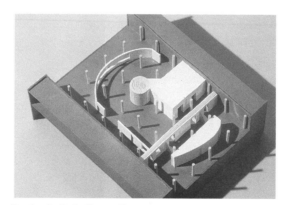

Project 4 Collage Space
The model was interpreted as space for a gallery from the collage drawing. This particular translation moved the project directly into the articulation of programmed spaces.

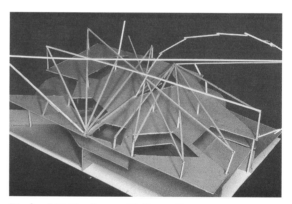

Project 5 Duchamp Collage Space
An interpretive concept model was made from the collage.

Alternatives

Multiple Approaches

Strategy

Whatever stage of development the project is investigating, distinctly different approaches should be explored to generate ideas and potential directions. This implies the construction of multiple sketch models. Models can, in turn, be selected from the alternative approaches and used for further study. As the project develops, alternatives may include ways to handle certain sections or building details. Composite models can also be made that incorporate ideas from different explorations.

Illustrations

In the first project, multiple sketch models were constructed to explore several directions.

In the following four projects, various approaches were taken to produce multiples. Whereas Projects 2 and 3 are similar to Project 1 in exploring different approaches, Projects 4 and 5 look at alternative refinements to a single scheme.

Project 1—First Alternative
The model approaches the project as a formal assemblage.

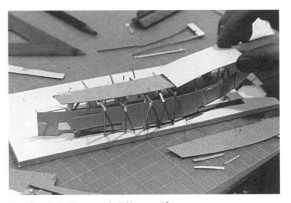

Project 1—Second Alternative
A linear organizational element in the form of a curved wall is used.

Project 1—Third Alternative
The project is explored as an elevated solution.

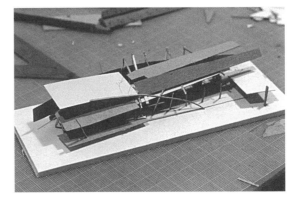

Project 1—Fourth Alternate
Uses the second alternative as a basis to mutate the design in another direction.

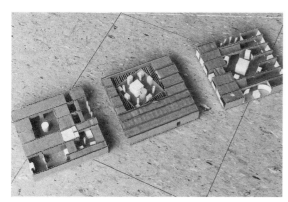

Project 2–Three Schemes

The models illustrate three different but related studies, produced to explore formal proportioning and alignment of space.

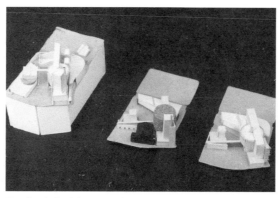

Project 3–Three Schemes

Three different schemes have been generated to explore possible directions for a project. The project is illustrated through all its phases under "Focusing: Mixed Use Complex" in this chapter.

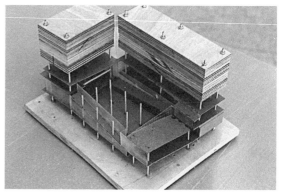

Project 5–Alternate Variations

These two alternatives are similar in approach and represent refinements to the design, as opposed to completely different directions.

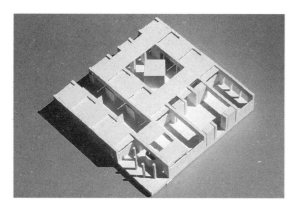

Project 2–Development Model

The model is a refinement of the models above, but rather than selecting one for further study, it combines aspects of all three models.

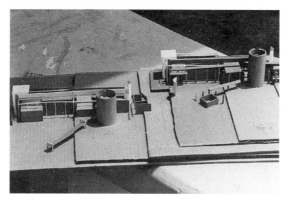

Project 4–Development Model Alternatives

These development models explore closely related variations of a single scheme. As such, this study indicates the kind of alternatives that might be explored after an initial direction is set.

Project 5–Alternative Variations

Although the project is strong at this level of finish, it may be more efficient to record changes with photography rather than completely rebuild the model.

Adjustable Models

Strategy

Another method for exploring alternative approaches is to construct models with components that can be adjusted to test various arrangements. Changes to the models may be recorded with a camera. This method of recording alternatives can also work well when making significant changes to a conventional sketch or development model.

Adjustable models are set up so that each component can be repositioned. This type of model is built with a deep, open base to allow columns to be pushed or pulled through the base. The holes for columns should be cut tightly so that friction will arrest the movement at the desired points. By moving the columns up and down, it is possible to examine the elements in a variety of attitudes.

Illustration

The models depict an alternative exploration method that allows components such as roof planes to be varied in relationship to each other without the designer's having to build multiple models.

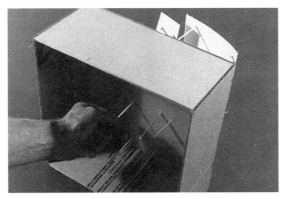

Roof Relationships
This ⅛″ = 1′-0″ scale model was built to study and fine-tune the relationships between a series of intersecting roof planes.

The model is turned up to expose the tails of the controlling sticks beneath. Pulling or pushing on the sticks changes the attitude of the roof, which can be considered in an infinite number of increments. *Note:* It can be helpful when fine-tuning roof attitudes to include perimeter walls, but in some cases this may inhibit the ability to alter relationships.

Roof Relationships
The initial setting of roof planes. *Note:* Straight pins have been used to attach the museum board to the balsa sticks. If the pins interfere with adjustments, they can be trimmed with side cutting pliers or electrical dykes.

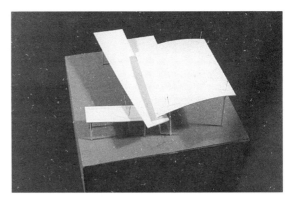

Roof Relationships
This setting displays the roof planes in a new attitude. *Note:* It is also possible to remove the sticks and change heights and/or stacking order.

Site

Contour Models

Strategy

Exploration should include the impact of the site on design decisions from the earliest stages. The construction of a contour model is an effective way to consider alternative site relationships.

Sketch contour models can be built of chipboard, scrap corrugated cardboard, and other inexpensive materials. They should be assembled with the idea that their reason for existence is to be cut into and modified in a number of ways. Presentation contour models are constructed with the use of similar methods, but differ in their use of materials.

Typical studies employing the contour model include exploring

- The building's scale in relation to the land mass
- How the building will knit into the site through devices such as grade changes and retaining walls
- Landscaping elements such as drives, walks, and other outdoor spaces

Illustration

The examples show two common types of contour models. For building demonstrations and discussion, see Chapter 2, "Solid Contour Model," and "Hollow Contour Model."

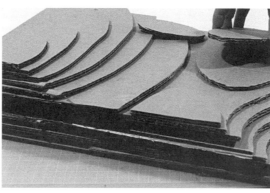

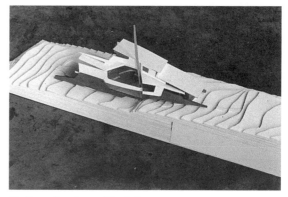

Solid Contour Models

Solid constructions are versatile and stable. One of their main advantages is that they can easily be cut on and patched. This makes them ideal for experimenting with grades and site designs as the project evolves.

Because the layers go all the way across their grade level, any cut into the grades will pass through the layers below. This makes it very easy to keep track of the effects of changes by counting contours.

Hollow Contour Models

Hollow models use less material and can be added to existing models. They can be difficult to modify, as any cut through the contours reveals the space below and must be patched. They are also less durable than solid models.

The model below has been built as a partial solid/hollow model. As the site gets progressively steep, solid sections can be stepped up to include only those areas where alterations are likely to occur. *Note:* Panels at the rear of the model reveal the hollow section.

Context Models

Strategy

For all projects, especially sites in an urban environment, it is necessary to construct at least the neighboring context buildings early in the investigation. By representing them in some form, the project scale and relation between buildings can begin to be understood.

Illustration

Models ranging from a large urban area to an immediate site are shown. *Note:* The context is treated as an abstract mass to allow the new work to be easily apprehended.

Neighboring Context
Neighboring structures have been built from neutral-colored corrugated cardboard as simple mass models in order to reveal the new building's relationship with the existing fabric.

Large Urban Context
Buildings have been cut from wood blocks as simple masses and painted flat gray as a non-competing background. The building site has been left as a level space so that different models can be placed on the site.

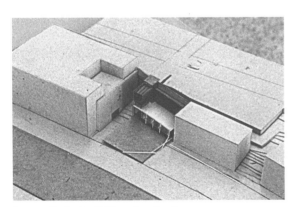

Immediate Building Context
The adjacent buildings on this site are critical to understanding the nature of the project, as they actually define the space of the site.

Immediate Building Context
Adjacent buildings have been built with less detail to serve as context for the new addition (light wood), and gray paint helps to code and downplay them.

Context Model in Progress
An urban context model in the process of construction is shown. Massing models of surrounding buildings have been cut from wood blocks and placed on the topographic map over their respective footprints.

Manipulation
Modifying and Editing

Strategy

Equally important to creating the model is the act of operating on it to discover and refine ideas. Modifications are most effective if the model is cut into and explored without the designer's becoming unduly concerned about its appearance or original configuration. If design operations appear to be difficult to implement, rough cutting will help establish the initial idea, and the resulting jagged surfaces can then be "cleaned up" once the idea is developed.

This type of investigation is important, because many of the design decisions cannot be visualized until the model is established. A number of ideas will be suggested by the model itself, and the new readings may prove more interesting than the original construction.

Illustration

Two projects have been modified and illustrate the kind of investigations that may be carried out at different stages of model evolution. The sketch model is still in the process of formation and can undergo radical transformations before moving on to the development model stage. The development model has reached the point where major relationships have been established and individual sections of the model can be modified and reformed.

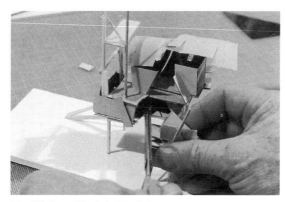

Modifying Sketch Models
A sketch model has been used as a working site and is radically altered to discover other relationships. The process was initiated by cutting completely through the model along a selected bias.

Modifying Development Models
One of the models shown in Chapter 1, "Model Types/Development Models," was used to refine the exterior wall relationship. At this point the previous wall components have been taken off and new cuts have been made directly on the model.

Modifying Sketch Models
The resultant halves were reassembled in a new relationship. This assemblage was used to visualize new components, which were then quickly cut and tested for successful integration.

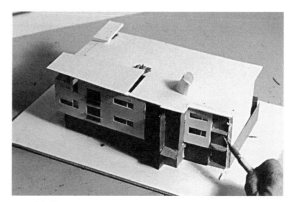

Modifying Development Models
The wall area has been rebuilt in a new but related configuration to refine this section of the design.

Modifying Site Contours

Strategy

Experimentation should be carried out on the site in a similar manner as on the building. Solid contour models made from inexpensive materials such as chipboard or corrugated cardboard are ideal for these studies. Grades can be cut out or added to accommodate a variety of conditions. As you experiment with various landscape treatments, it is helpful to save removed contour material so that it can be replaced for alternative solutions.

Modifications also can be made to hollow models, but new contours must be attached to fill the holes left by cutting into the model.

TYPICAL MODIFICATIONS

- Creating a level grade for the building
- Creating drives and walks that cut into or rise above existing grades
- Creating cuts through several grades where soil must be retained (This typically occurs along property lines where changes are made.)
- Creating terraces, berms, or drainage swales

Illustration

The images on the right show cardboard study models used to explore grade changes for drives, walks, and buildings. The images on the far right are of sites made from malleable materials that can be molded as desired.

Contour Model Changes
Contours are cut for an entry drive in the model. Slopes can be calculated by counting contours and the distance to the next level. The model is ⅛ in. scale. Each contour = 1'-0', so 10 ft forward produces a 1 in 10 slope.

Study Model with Grade Changes
Areas with two or more contours cut down will require retaining walls. *Note:* Bad cuts can be reversed by simply replacing material. Rough splice lines will not matter in this experimental phase.

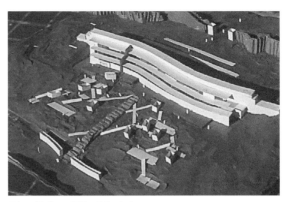

Plasticine Site Model
Grades and leveled areas for building footprints can easily be molded from this claylike material. Grades have the advantage of smooth appearance, but it is difficult to transfer the contours to drawings.

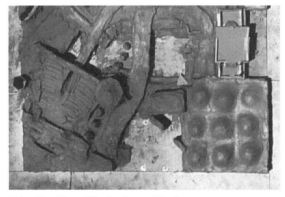

Plastic Clay Study for a Park
This material can be quickly formed and is conducive to exploring alternatives. *Note:* As in the preceding example, it can be difficult to transfer final grades accurately to drawings, and achieving crisp edge definition is challenging.

Digression

Strategy

Often in the course of exploration, new directions emerge that do not follow the original intention. Instead of ignoring these and steering the design along preconceived paths, it can be profitable to let go of earlier ideas and follow the implications suggested by the model. This may involve following the design through a strong shift in direction or even returning to an earlier generation in preference to later versions. Readings that emerge from rough studies or poorly crafted models such as warped, off-center, or overlapping materials, can be adopted as a discoveries and are often more interesting than the intended readings.

Illustration

The sketch model and the subsequent finish model on the right demonstrate the tendency to regularize anomalies in the model in keeping with intended readings. This is a case in which it can be argued that the earlier exploration was potentially more interesting than the "tightened up" finish model.

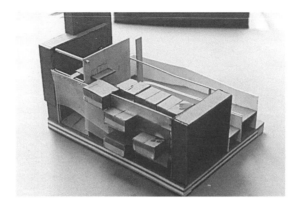

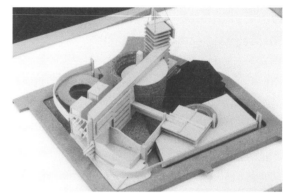

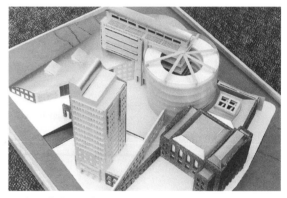

Using Accidents

The thin acetate wall on the front of this sketch model displays a degree of unintentional warping and curvature that is potentially interesting. Although it is not the actual second stage for the project, the model below is typical of the regularization applied to make the model conform to preconceptions. The results can be less interesting than the "accidents" suggested by the rough sketch. For this reason, it can be useful to let the project evolve on its own and take advantage of unintended discoveries.

Maintaining Discovery

A form of reverse digression can occur in which the model discoveries are lost in the translation to a higher level of refinement. In this example, many ideas developed in earlier stages have been "normalized" in moving to the presentation level. The loss of discovery is similar in effect to a failure to use accidents. In both cases, regularizing tendencies and unwillingness to let the model guide the evolution of the project have displaced some interesting ideas.

Interpreting

Strategy

Sometimes manipulation can be a matter of making a fundamental shift in either the model or the designer's perception of the model. This can be accomplished by using a number of processes. Processes can be combined or modified to generate other approaches based on your own exploration.

Illustration

The examples represent several typical strategies. They are similar in nature to concept models and are offered as experimental approaches to stimulate ideas.

The study models typically used to explore various strategies employ quick-assembly techniques and offer the designer freedom to experiment without becoming unduly attached to the product.

The final set of projects includes concept models paired with models that extract a reading from them to create an architectural space. These models provide a link between the abstract, conceptual nature of models used to generate ideas and models that begin translating ideas into integrated building designs.

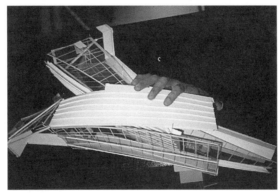

Fragment

A section of a large model has been severed from its original context and placed in a new attitude. This fragment is then reinterpreted as a complete building. By exploring new attitudes, several different solutions to the project are suggested.

Recycling

Another example that expands on the idea of fragments is to treat parts from previous models as found objects. By building a large inventory of cast-off project pieces, you can rethink and cross-assemble them. With modifications and the introduction of new elements, a number of ideas can be produced in short order.

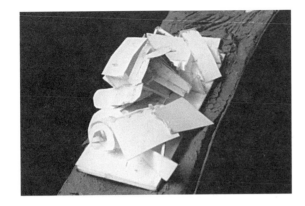

Distortion

The models have been intentionally crushed and distorted by applying pressure at one location with a flat surface. The resulting geometry offers a number of new readings that carry the internal logic of their initial relationships.

Sectioning

The model is transformed by cutting it into two parts along a carefully selected bias line. The resulting parts are then realigned along a new axis and stitched together. The resulting formation is used to generate ideas based on the implications of space, form, and structural demands.

The model can also be sectioned and used to discover new relationships based on the internal order revealed by the cut.

Scale Shift

A section of the ⅛″ = 1′-0″ scale model (shown below) has been identified with particularly interesting relationships. This section was isolated and reinterpreted at four times its original size. The new model is now taken to represent the same square footage as the original project, and the program is reinserted into it.

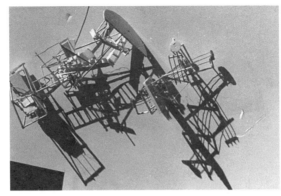

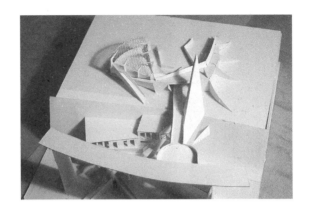

Superimposition

The model can be photographed as double exposures, and new images can be discovered in the resulting overlay. Although it may be difficult to see the finer transparencies in the reproduction above, the bolder suggestion of form overlaid on form should be evident.

The model below is superimposed on an image of circus animals and offers a comingling of cross-cultural relations. The kind of interpretative selection process that this exercise requires is similar to that used for collage drawings and axonometric overlays.

Projecting

An interesting exercise for generating new ideas involves the use of three-dimensional forms to produce two-dimensional images. The shadows thrown off by the objects are best experimented with at lower sun or artificial light angles. The models can be turned in many directions to explore various types of shadow patterns. The patterns can be interpreted to create new models and models can in turn generate successive 2-D patterns through a reflexive interchange of information.

Axonometric

The process involves a dialogue between the drawing and the model and is related to the topics discussed in "Working with Concept Drawings" in this chapter. It is initiated by overlaying several outline drawings and extruding selected elements upward at varying heights to create a three-dimensional axonometric drawing. The drawing is then interpreted as a building and invested with program, site considerations, and structure to produce the model. The process becomes more controllable after experimenting several times.

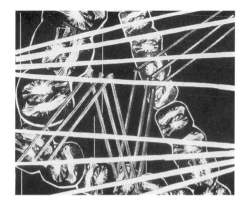

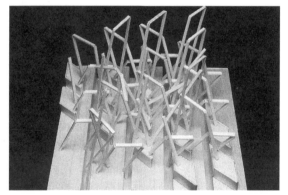

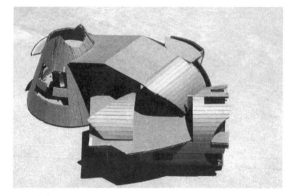

Collage

To begin, a collage is created by manipulating a set of base images from any number of sources. A model is then made based on the collage. The model will most likely become a concept model, but interpretations can convert the ideas directly into a building scheme. Part of this process is controlled by the nature of the drawing. Repetitive images are less likely to lend themselves to the hierarchy of programmatic issues. For possible variations on the collage approach, see "Working with Concept Drawings" earlier in this chapter.

Collision

Two strategies employing the idea of collision are shown. Both are initiated in model form. The model above was started by building two open "wire frame" forms of contrasting sizes and shapes and engaging the two parts. The resultant collision can be used to make decisions about what is solid and open and how programming might be accommodated.

The model below uses a similar approach, but the three forms used for collision were solid masses carved away to create the voids. Intersections offer the most potential.

Intervention/Rotation

Intervention is similar in concept to collision. A regular field such as a grid or other repetitive pattern is established as the ground or field. A form "alien" in size and shape is then imposed in the body of the pattern at some disruptive or rotated angle. The resultant space is interpreted to accommodate architectural considerations. The diagram above illustrates the basic idea. The model below is a building developed by imposing a curved gesture on an existing grid structure.

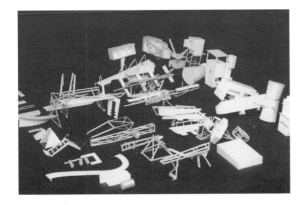

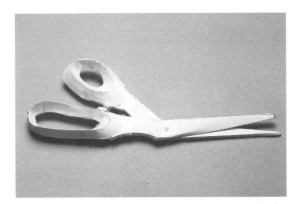

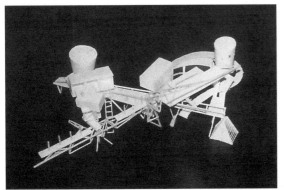

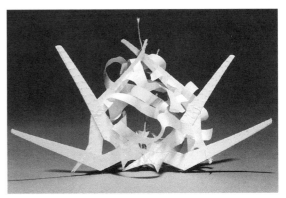

Lexicon

This process is related to recycling elements; however, rather than using existing elements, a vocabulary (or lexicon) of new parts is generated. The elements can be created as a number of platonic forms with variations. The parts for this example were generated by designing seven kiosks and then disassembling them. Many elements were used to create a critical mass capable of producing unpredictable combinations. The model below was one of dozens made from combining the various elements.

Repetitive Frames

This process involves the use of a repeated element to form an architecturally designed armature. To begin, a single frame is designed with a target height and span in mind. The frame is stressed by pressing on key points, and ideas for modifications are incorporated to reinforce structural weak points. The frame is repeated to describe an area of space and becomes the structural skeleton for a building. In the example below, the frames have been roofed and glazed to develop a small airport terminal.

Patterning

The process is initiated by cutting parts to cover an ordinary object, like those used for making garment patterns. The object should be complex, as opposed to a platonic form such as a cylinder. The pieces are then disassembled and used in a similar manner to the "lexicon" strategy to make a concept model. In this case the vocabulary was expanded to include multiples of selected parts. The process can be extended to producing drawings from the models. See "Working with Concept Drawings" earlier in this chapter.

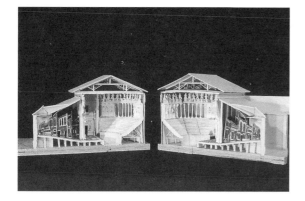

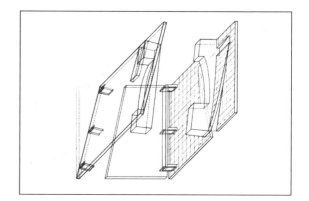

Precedent Interpretation

This strategy is shown in four frames and is initiated by using an existing architecture as a ground for study and interpretation. In this example the Teatro Olimpico in Vicenza, Italy, was built in model form and then cut into two sections with a band saw. The sections were carefully studied with drawings (not shown) and translated into interpretive ideas about space using the study models below. The process then proceeded to a fifth and sixth stage, shown in the following frames.

Precedent Interpretation

Ideas from the study models in the previous frames were selected and combined to produce a spatial interpretation with the hydrocal (plaster) model shown above. The space discovered in this model was then studied in drawing form on an experiential level, that is, as a projection of what the experience might be like moving through the space. For related topics, see "Working with Concept Drawings" in Chapter 3 and "Casting Molds" in Chapter 5.

Cartesian Transformation

Transformation, or the manipulation of existing orders, can be carried out in many ways. One method is to establish a gridded cube in drawing form. The faces of the cube are then rotated at various angles, and decisions are made about pushing and pulling forms from them. Once under way, a three-dimensional interpretation is established and suggests moves that can be pursued on the model. See "Working with Concept Drawings" earlier in this chapter.

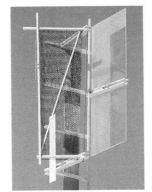

Concept Model and Interior Space

The proportion and movement study above is translated into the space below using the flowing lines of the concept model to inform the elevations and sections.

Concept Model and Building

The shade, light, and shadow device shown above has been translated into ideas that inform the shading elements and the geometry of the beach pavilion below.

Diagram Model and Building

The geometry of the building follows the basic direction set by the diagram model in orchestrating the play between a strong central axis and the wandering quality of the intersecting wall as it moves across the site.

Development

Project Development

The development process is central to the use of a model as a design tool. The approaches discussed in the sections "Ideas" and "Manipulation" are applied, using study models in a chain of evolutionary stages. This process is similar to two-dimensional design evolution in that concepts are used to develop schemes and are integrated with structure, site, and programming issues to produce a complete architecture. The process relies on the interrelated concepts of "increasing scale" and "focusing" (discussed later in this chapter) as methods for advancement and is reinforced by "coding and hierarchy of materials" and the "converting" techniques also discussed later in the chapter.

Illustration

An abbreviated model progression with four stages of refinement bridges the gap between the single-stage interpretations of concept models (shown previously) and the expanded set of model stages in "Focusing," presented later in this chapter.

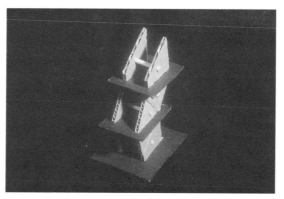

Retreat Stage 1
The project explores themes from the play *Eleemosynary* to design a retreat for Echo, a primary character in the play. The study employs a simple harmonica as its initial design generator.

Retreat Stage 2
A sketch model is used to develop spatial organizations and site engagement, using the conceptual tectonic system as a basis for decisions.

Retreat Stage 3
The concept model is used to develop a basic tectonic system.

Retreat Stage 4
The study is increased in scale and focus to develop the ideas into the retreat for Echo. The final project can be seen to effectively integrate ideas from the isolated study models.

Increasing Scale
Sketch, Development, and Finish Models

Strategy

As a model evolves, it is typical to increase its size, moving from general relationships to greater levels of detail. This process of starting small and moving up in scale is analogous to focusing a lens. At low powers, the lens sees only general shapes and gestures. As greater focal powers are applied, elements become increasingly defined until details are clearly apprehended. See "Scale" in Chapter 3.

Illustration

In the examples to the right, the initial sketch models were established at small scales. As the direction became more focused, the scale was increased to develop more detailed readings.

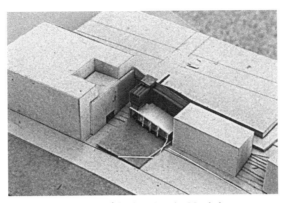

Project A–Initial ¹/₃₂ in. Scale Model
A project investigation looking at overall issues of scale, massing, and mechanics of the scheme with a small ¹⁄₃₂" = 1'-0" sketch model.

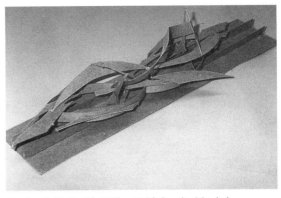

Project B–Initial 1" = 50' Scale Model
Project investigation looking at overall issues of gesture, flow, and spatial layering.

Project A–¹/₈ in. Development Model
With the direction of overall issues established, the model is enlarged by a factor of four to ¹⁄₈" = 1'-0" to facilitate a higher level of focus.

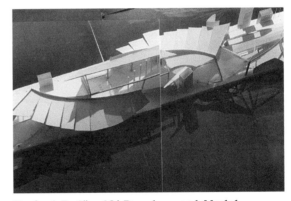

Project B–1" = 10' Development Model
An increase in scale to 1" = 10', which considers the articulation of components, refines relationships, and further develops the play between program and structure.

Increasing Scale
Development and Finish Models
Illustration

The two development models to the right take the idea of scaling to the next level of focus. By increasing the scale of isolated sections, exploration and refinement continue to evolve.

Development Model

The building has been articulated to a certain level of resolution, but an important area of the project at the center of the circular field requires further study.

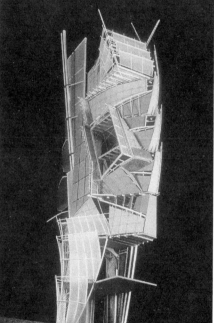

Development Section

The area at the center of the circular field has been increased in scale to study its elements with more precision.

Finish and Development Model

A section from the finish model above has been isolated and scaled up (below) to develop the facade elements. See "Focusing" later in this chapter.

Increasing Scale

Building Interior Models

Strategy

Part of the process of increasing scale involves enlarging the model to be able to focus on interior components. Such models typically function as development models and are constructed to study interior architectural spaces and mill work.

Interior models are typically built at scales of ¼″ = 1′-0″ and larger if possible. These models must define the borders of the space but remain open for viewing and working room.

Illustration

The models to the right demonstrate typical scales and treatments for interior models.

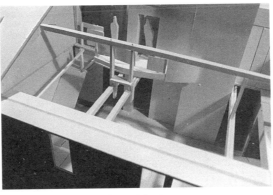

½ in. House Interiors Study

This ½″ = 1′-0″ scale foam core model employs a removable roof for viewing. Components were developed directly inside the model. *Note:* The scale is large enough to read details as small as 1 in.

¼ in. House Interiors Study

Existing ¼″ = 1′-0″ scale models such as this are often large enough to develop interior partitions and circulation elements.

½ in. Scale Section Study

An interior development model of a unit in a multifamily building has been built at a ½″ = 1′-0″ scale to develop interior components.

½ in. Atrium/Lobby Study

This ½ in. scale development model was used to add, remove, and refine various elements for an atrium space. Portions of the rough model were recut after alterations were made.

Increasing Scale

Detail Models

Strategy

As project development proceeds, models are built at even larger scales to develop details such as window treatments, railings, facias, and so forth.

These models are treated in a similar manner as building models but are built at much larger scales to study the finer readings of form articulation and connections.

Scales typically range from ½" = 1'-0" to 3" = 1'-0". Detail models can be helpful in resolving design ideas and construction details and in facilitating client communication.

Illustration

The detail models on the right demonstrate ways in which the model can be used to develop details or special furnishings.

Window Surround

This museum board and foam core model was built at a relatively large 3" = 1'-0" scale to study relationships between corner connections and wall depth. *Note:* Test angles have been cut to fit the curved corners together.

Table

This 1" = 1'-0" scale foam core model was used to develop a small table. Detail models are also useful for the study of interior elements such as cabinets and built-in shelving.

Fireplace/Waterfall

These relatively small ¼" = 1'-0" sketch models were used to develop designs for a fireplace/fountain. *Note:* As typical of developing designs, three alternative solutions were constructed.

Library Kiosk

This small study for a movable book carrel was built at ½" = 1'-0" scale, and its parts could be turned to explore the effect of shades and adjustable racks.

Coding and Hierarchy of Materials

Strategy

It is effective to use different materials based on classifications of building elements, such as exterior walls and interior partitions. This type of coding reinforces the ability to "read," or understand, the project's defining elements and geometries. It also begins to convey the sense of weight various elements will project both in terms of their relative importance and physical heaviness.

As projects become further resolved, components should reflect the actual scale thickness of walls, roofs, slabs, and beams. This hierarchical range adds a level of contrasting elements and makes the model convincing as an architectural representation.

Illustration

The following projects use a range of scales and color to reflect different component types.

The two illustrations at the bottom of the page demonstrate the practice of detailing edges to reflect their true scaled thickness. *Note:* As a model is scaled up, it will not present a contrasting range of elements and can appear unconvincing if the thicknesses of modeling sheets do not accurately reflect the true scale of the elements.

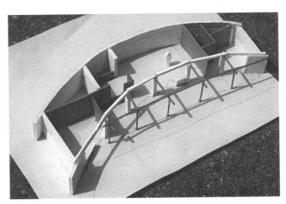

Coded Structure

The structure of this ⅛" = 1′0″ scale house model is made up of 8 in. concrete masonry units and internally divided with wood-framed walls. All members representing the masonry elements have been constructed from 3⁄16 in. foam core. Interior partition walls and exterior trellis components are cut from chipboard. Beams over front wall openings have been cut to scale.

Coded Materials and Concept

The coding of this model can be read in two ways. The material of the central datum wall, the dark box behind it, and the translucent screen wall in front, all convey a sense of contrasting color, weight, and material. Alternately, the conceptual organization anchored by the central wall with adjoining components is clearly delineated.

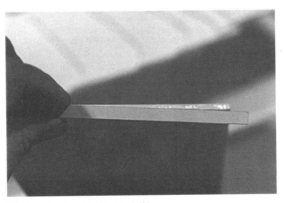

¼ in. Scale Facia Detail

A ⅛ in. foam core roof plane is edged with a 10 in. scaled strip of museum board.

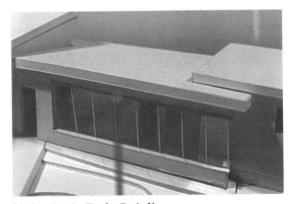

¼ in. Scale Facia Detail

The edge of the roof now reflects the true 10 in. depth of the facia.

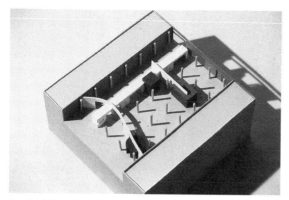

Coded Program Components

A clear delineation is made between the program components by coding the interior of the space gray, circulation elements in white, and program spaces in dark board.

Coded Buildings and Addition

The model components for the addition use coding to differentiate between the dark-colored existing building and the new elements.

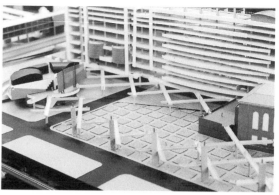

Coding Planing Elements

In this model, buildings, site elements, and tectonic constructions such as the unifying trellis work have all been coded with a range of materials to clearly differentiate the parts of the complex.

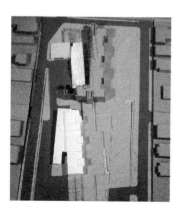

Coded Site Components

The site is coded to differentiate the ground plane, roads, existing buildings, and new structures (in white). *Note:* The site and existing buildings are in darker neutral tones and allow the new work to stand out.

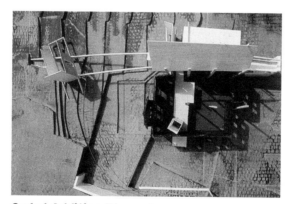

Coded Addition Elements

The difference between the dark walls of the existing building and the new components, intervening through its space, can be clearly read because of the contrasting materials.

Coded Structure and Organization

White anchor and circulation elements, gray board walls, and wood structural gridding have been used to reinforce structural systems and program organization.

Converting
Renovating Models
Strategy

Although there is a point when many decisions have been made and a model has to be recrafted, models are often needlessly rebuilt every time a few elements are changed. This can consume a lot of time. Instead, renovation techniques can be used effectively to clean up a model. In many cases the results of these techniques are entirely adequate for more formal presentations.

Illustration

The sketch model on the right is refaced to upgrade its level of finish. For complete step-by-step illustration of this project, see "Case Study B" in Chapter 4.

Models on the far right have been covered in paper to code and upgrade their level of finish.

Project A Renovation

A typical refacing begins by cutting openings in an overlay sheet. This method is more practical than cutting holes through the model. Transfer tape is used for surfaces likely to warp if glue is applied.

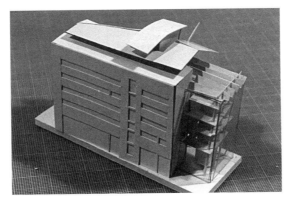

Project A Renovation

The resultant understated shadow lines generally read better on small models as visual layers. Additional facings can be cut and applied over all the original cuts to continue elevating the model's finish.

Project B Covering with Paper

Colored paper can be used to renovate or code the model's surface. Paper can be attached with Spray Mount or double-face transfer tape. Glue sticks can be used on the edges.

Project C Site Renovation

Site surfaces can be covered with paper to smooth out contours on rough models. The paper helps to visually reduce the large change in contours on the initial model and serves to elevate the level of finish.

Focusing

Strategy

Focusing refers to the application of evolutionary stages of development. It draws on all the ideas presented in this chapter and is central to the process of moving a project from a germ of an idea through successive stages of refinement. The process may begin with alternatives and digression, but as it evolves, each new model builds on the generalized relationships of the previous stage to arrive at an integrated building design.

Typical Evolutionary Stages

Proceeding from initial information

- To alternate concept and sketch studies
- To fixed geometry and relationships
- To exploring alternative treatments
- To looking at alternative detailing
- To a resolved project design

Illustration

The projects on the following pages illustrate the model stages used in the evolutionary chain of model progression. Although individual projects do not employ every strategy, taken together they illustrate examples of all the primary ideas and can be applied collectively in a comprehensive process of investigation.

College Complex

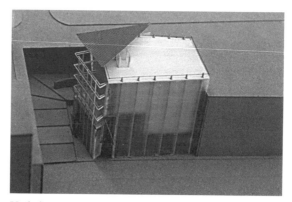

Hotel

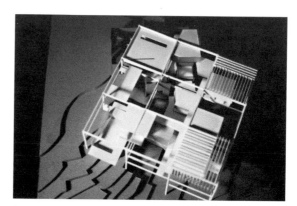

Faculty Center

Library

Mixed-Use Project

College Complex

This project presents several strong aspects of modeling. They include development of conceptual ideas through successive stages and the use of the model to develop the facade and elevations. See "Increasing Scale," earlier in this chapter.

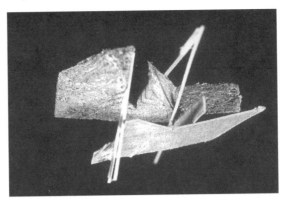

College Complex Stage 1
The development of dormitories, galleries, and art studios is initiated with a concept/gesture model to interpret the dichotomy between the suburban and urban landscapes.

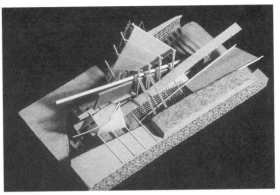

College Complex Stage 2
The relationship suggested by the concept model is engaged with the site. This sketch model serves to translate gestures into a building construct.

College Complex Stage 3
Growing out of the earlier discoveries, the program and other organizational issues are engaged for possible occupations on the site.

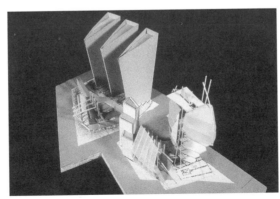

College Complex Stage 4
The overall organization and general form of the complex has been developed, and attention turns to refining the individual elements.

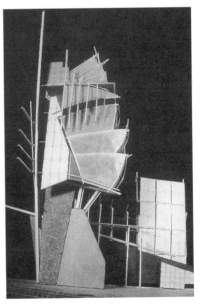

College Complex Stage 5
The tower is developed as a finish model. A section of the tower is then scaled up for more study. See Chapter 3 "Increasing Scale Development/Finish Models."

Library

This project presents several important strategies used to develop projects, beginning with the use of alternate schemes for the concept model. This can also be done when translating concept ideas into initial architectural issues, but should be employed at some point in the early stages of model progression.

After developing an initial scheme, scale may be increased to focus on a discrete section of the model. The earlier studies are then taken to the level of a development model. The development model is, in turn, refined and renovated to serve as the finish model.

Library Stage 1

The project is initiated with conceptual studies based on diagramming the site context. Three different readings of the site are made to explore alternatives.

Library Stage 2

An interpretation of the concept models is made to establish general ideas about organization, structure, and expression.

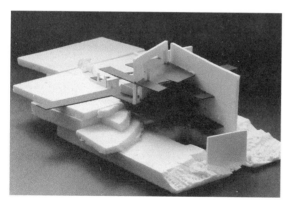

Library Stage 3

A critical area of the sketch model is increased in scale to work out such issues as sectional relationships, entry progression, and material hierarchy.

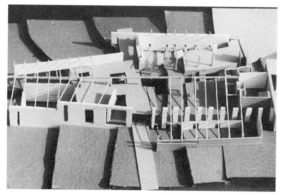

Library Stage 4

The study is expanded to the level of a development model, where issues are further refined on the model and in drawing form.

Library Stage 5

The final model uses the development model as its basis by renovating the site contours and adding components. Rather than rebuilding the model, time is used effectively to advance the exploration.

Hotel

This example demonstrates the strong use of early conceptual investigations and site engagement. The model chain exhibits the typical use of a development model to expand on the general themes of the sketch model.

Hotel Stage 1
The project is initiated with a concept model to investigate issues of materials and spatial readings.

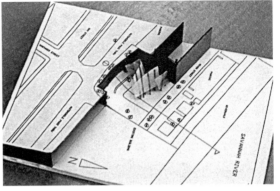

Hotel Stage 2
Early studies begin by translating investigations to the site and reading the relationships to establish a direction.

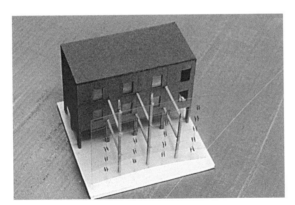

Hotel Stage 3
A scaled-up model is built to develop the material and transparency issues suggested by the previous studies.

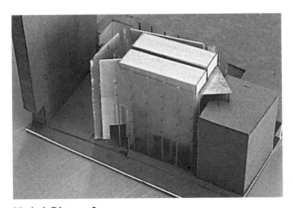

Hotel Stage 4
As ideas are developed, the model is increased in scale to focus on refining various passages.

Hotel Stage 5
Connections, detailing, and other issues are developed on a presentation model.

Faculty Center

The stages in the evolution of this model are informative as they explore two alternate schemes, then combine them to establish the basis for the architecture.

The project also illustrates how the designer can use the development model to maintain design focus by letting it serve as the final model, rather than rebuilding what has already been established.

Faculty Center Stage 1
The design is initiated with a sketch model, exploring strategies for the intervention of space on an existing ruin. In this scheme a super grid is proposed as a rational field passing through the ruins.

Faculty Center Stage 2
A separate approach is explored with another sketch model, using a sectional stacking of planes to define space and engage the body of the ruins.

Faculty Center Stage 3
The grid scheme and stacked planes are combined in a sketch/development model. At this stage, ideas of program and circulation are used to order spaces.

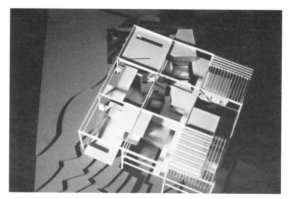

Faculty Center Stage 4
The development model has been used for exploration all the way through the project. To bring the model to the level of a finished study, sections have been altered and rebuilt as needed.

Mixed-Use Complex

Several strategies have been used in evolving this project. A concept/diagram model and context study are used to generate initial information, then three sketch models are used to translate the raw concepts into alternative building propositions. By beginning with the three small sketches, then moving to a development model, increasing scale for a finish model, and finally scaling up the structure of the circular building, four levels of scaled models can be observed at work.

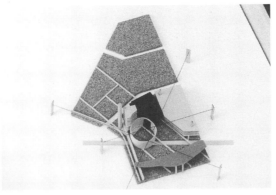

Mixed-Use Complex Stage 1

The project is initiated with a conceptual diagram of the site to generate physical ideas based on relationships between the overlaying forces and existing structures.

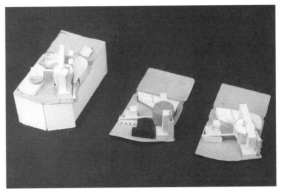

Mixed-Use Complex Stage 2

Ideas from the initial investigation are used to explore three different organizational schemes.

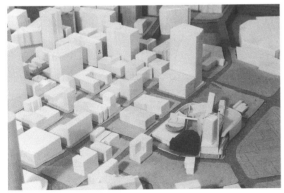

Mixed-Use Complex Stage 3

Schemes are tested in the context of the site as they are developed.

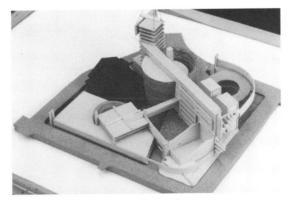

Mixed-Use Complex Stage 4

A scheme is selected and refined at a larger scale with a development model.

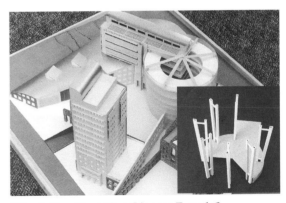

Mixed-Use Complex Stages 5 and 6

The development study is increased in scale and detailed to produce the finish model. The circular structural system is also scaled up and studied to develop details.

APPLY

Step-by-Step Case Studies
of Concepts and Techniques

The following projects trace the evolution of
five designs from early conceptual stages to
finish models. Many assembly techniques and
strategies presented in Chapters 2 and 3 are
shown to convey possible applications in the
context of evolving designs.

Case Study A
Residence
Stage 1—Initial Sketch Studies

Strategy

With the project parameters in mind, the designer makes alternative sketch models from small schematic scaled drawings and pencil sketches. After exploring different approaches to generate ideas, an individual or hybrid model is selected for further development.

Assembly

Rapid construction techniques using knife, scissors, and hot glue

Project

A 2,000 sq ft house on a narrow infill lot

Scale $\frac{1}{16}'' = 1'\text{-}0''$

Models measure approximately $2'' \times 3''$ (actual size) and are kept small for initial studies. *Note:* Even at this scale, the model is not built as a pure massing model but is treated as a solid/void model to understand the contribution of openings to the overall composition of forms.

Materials

- Poster board
- $\frac{1}{16}$ in. foam core

Illustration

Five alternative approaches are made to generate ideas and explore a range of directions. Work is begun using small measured schematic drawings, with each model employing a basic formal strategy to organize its moves.

Alternative 1

This scheme is organized as a linear grouping. It is readily apparent that the program will need a second story to preserve any yard space.

Alternative 2

This scheme concentrates the program on the second level in another linear side-loaded organization, based on Alternative 1.

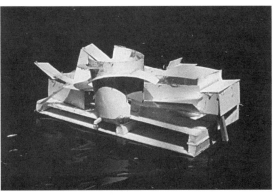

Alternative 3

This scheme uses a central drum as the focal point for its organization and covers the entire buildable area with a single-story solution.

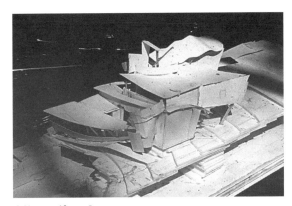

Alternative 4

This scheme engages two volumes with all other spaces expanding from them. With modifications, this scheme is selected for further study with a development model. See Case Study A, Stage 2, in Chapter 4.

Alternative 5

This scheme employs a courtyard defined by a second-story bridge.

Stage 2—Manipulation and Focusing

Strategy

The general direction of the sketch is increased in scale for further study and development. Alternative solutions for different sections of the model are also considered.

Assembly

The model is assembled with relative speed, but more accurately than the sketch model. Parts are lightly adhered using white glue with the intent of cutting and changing the components as the model progresses. A number of building and editing techniques are illustrated during the construction of this model.

Project

A 2,000 sq ft house on a narrow infill lot

Scale ⅛″ = 1′-0″

The scale of the sketch model is doubled in size for this study. The increase allows for more detail and refinement but is still small enough to lend itself to quick alterations and visualization.

Materials

■ Two-ply museum board paper

Illustration

Alternative three is selected from the initial studies and rebuilt for further study. The raised section at the rear of the initial model is immediately lowered to the ground plane. This "tail" is then modified several times to explore different readings.

At this level of study, the development model must show all solid/void relationships to provide the next level of information.

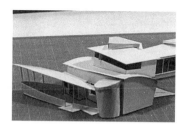

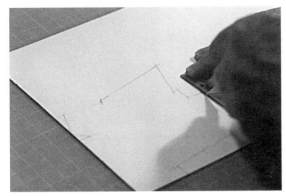

1. The plan is transferred with a knife to the base sheet. *Note:* Although scaled plans should yield accurate parts, adjustments must be made to compensate for the thickness of materials and to conform to small variations that occur in the actual model.

2. Walls are erected and small parts put in place with the aid of a knife point.

3. The shape of the conical stair tower roof is templated directly from the model. Because this shape varies in its rate of curvature, direct templating is one of the most dependable ways to achieve an accurate fit.

4. The second story is held in place to make a rough template for the curving roof plane.

5. A finished roof is made by adjusting the rough template and recutting the part until an exact fit can be achieved. *Note:* For forms that change geometry in three dimensions, it is difficult to cut shapes that will fit perfectly the first time.

6. An initial "tail" wing is tacked together with a glue gun.

7. The tail is edited by cutting with scissors.

8. Openings are cut directly on the model. *Note:* If needed, these can be cut accurately by using a small triangle to guide the knife edge (see Case Study B in Chapter 4).

9. The resultant openings with small shading additions.

10. A wedge is cut out of the box to try out another angle on the tail.

11. The move is rejected, and the wedge is reattached to the box. *Note:* It helps to save all parts that are cut off for replacement if the modifications are not satisfactory.

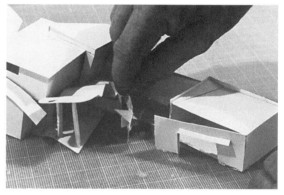

12. The walls of the tail are broken open to study the potential for other arrangements.

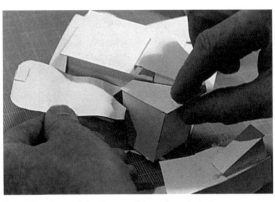

13. Using scissors to cut out small pieces directly on the model, attention is directed to developing the front of the building. *Note:* Attention should move around the model so that one area does not become overdeveloped in relation to other sections.

14. The knuckle formed by the stair tower between the main body and the tail is redesigned.

15. Returning to the rear of the model, a third alternate facade is considered, and the tail is rebuilt one more time. The final parts have been recut to match the level of finish on the other sections.

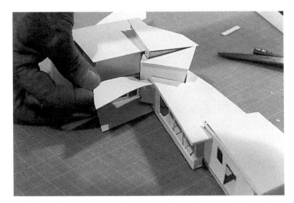

16. An alternate patio covering is considered as the investigation nears completion.

17. The completed development model is shown. *Note:* The site has not been addressed on this model, although it was included at the sketch model stage and has been explored in terms of the way the building will relate to it.

Stage 3—Finish Model and Site

Strategy

With the basic relationships established, the model is again increased in scale and built with greater accuracy.

The presentation/finish model can also be considered an advanced type of study model, as it affords the focus for designing details such as glazing patterns, site elements, interiors, and roof treatments.

Assembly

A number of new techniques and materials applicable to finish models are included in this example.

Project

A 2,000 sq ft house on a narrow infill lot

Scale ¼" = 1'-0"

This is a typical scale for fully developed house models, as it allows sufficient size for detailing.

Materials

- Three-ply museum board paper
- ³⁄₁₆ in. foam core

Illustration

The model is built as an example of the level of finish appropriate for formal presentations. The abstract detailing relies on implied material simulation. Items that cannot be reproduced accurately at ¼" = 1'-0" scale (less than 2 in.) are not included.

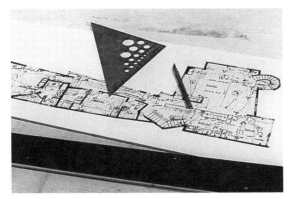

1. The surface of the model base is lightly scored by tracing a set of floor plans with a sharp knife. The plans have been spray mounted and are removed after the wall lines have been transferred. *Note:* Apply spray outdoors.

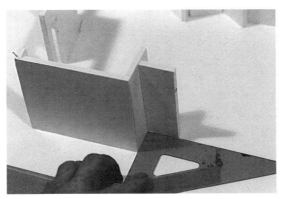

2. The plans have been removed, and the basement walls are laid out along the scored lines. A triangle is used to ensure accurate corner joints and vertical alignment of walls.

3. Wall connections are held together with straight pins. This speeds construction by allowing successive joints to be made without waiting for glue to dry. *Note:* Corner angles have been cut at 45 degrees to allow the paper to meet without exposing the Styrofoam core.

4. After the glue is dry, pins can be removed or pushed in if the heads are hidden by other parts of the model.

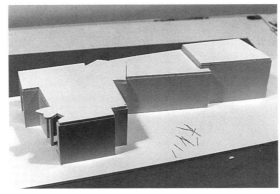

5. Completed basement and first floor are shown. *Note:* Site contours will be built up around the basement level.

6. Using drawings to template the facade, museum board is cut to include only the dominant mullion details.

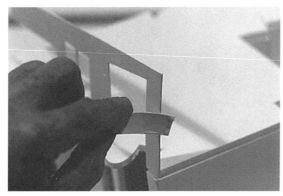

7. A thin line of white glue is applied directly to the wall edge.

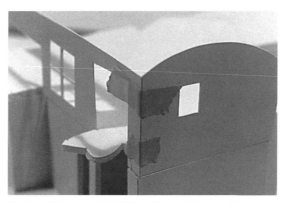

8. A wall joint is held in place with drafting tape until the glue can set.

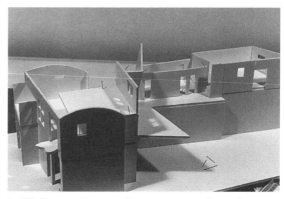

9. Walls continue to be constructed on the main floor of the house.

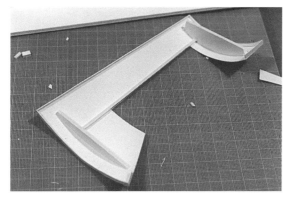

10. A rough curved roof is cut to determine fit, as demonstrated on the development model. The final cut for the roof is reinforced with hidden bracing to maintain radiuses at each end.

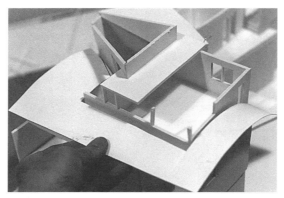

11. The roof is placed on the second floor. Supports allow the roof and the second floor to be taken off for viewing the interior of the model.

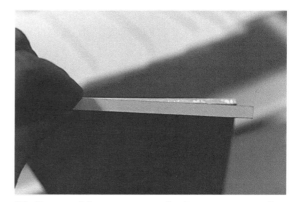

12. Exposed foam core roof edges are covered with museum board. *Note:* Edges should be scaled to their intended depth rather than letting the given thickness of the material remain inaccurately sized. In the example, edges have been cut to read 8 in. and 10 in. at scale.

13. A conical entry tower is made from museum board by rolling with a round marker.

14. Street face components of the first floor are assembled.

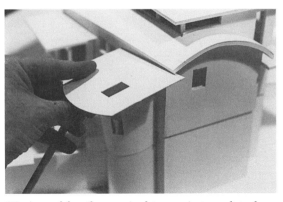

15. A roof for the conical tower is templated directly from the model, using discarded model material.

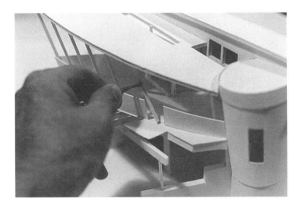

16. Detailing is added, with tweezers used to handle the finer elements.

17. The basic body of the model is completed and ready for the site contours. See "Work" in Chapter 2.

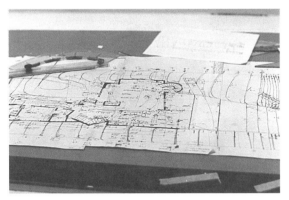

18. A hollow site contour model is constructed directly on the model by using a site drawing with 6 in. contours and ⅛ in. foam core. At ¼″ = 1′-0″ scale, each layer of foam core is equal to a 6 in. change in grade.

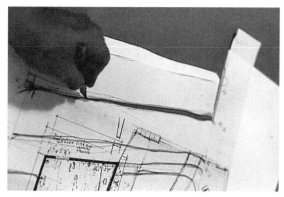

19. Contours are cut between the lines with a 1 in. projection beyond each contour to allow a tab for gluing the successive layers together.

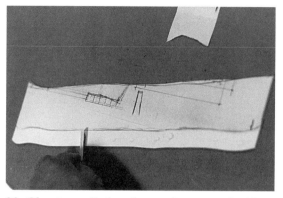

20. Glue is applied and spread out evenly. *Note:* The line of the contour above should be marked so that glue will not get on the material past this point and be exposed. The paper template can also be left on to protect this area until it is in place.

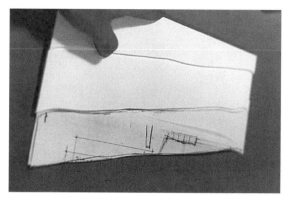

21. The overlapping contours are glued to the 1 in. projection on successive contours. *Note:* This type of site model can be built from the top down, instead of from the base up as in the solid contour model.

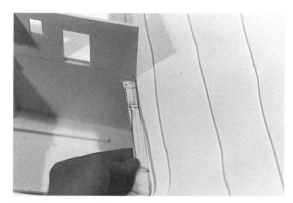

22. After several contours have been connected together, the section is supported from below and attached to the body of the building.

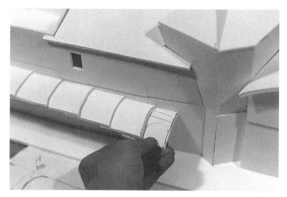

23. Individual contours are continued down the side of the house.

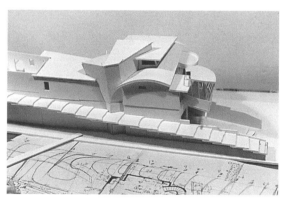

24. A completed side is shown.

25. The opposite side is completed, and a notch is cut for the location of the site stairs.

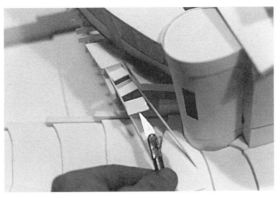

26. Site details and ancillary components such as the entry stairs can now be assembled.

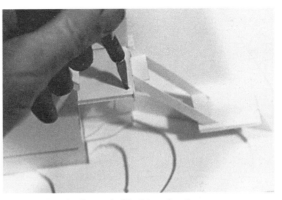

27. A pilot hole is drilled in the foam core, using the knife tip.

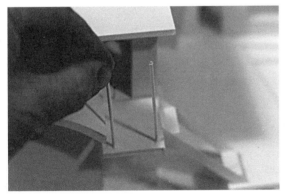

28. White plastic rods are cut and glued in the resulting sockets for canopy columns.

29. Foam core is cut down to the paper and scraped clean to hide the foam at the corner joints. *Note:* This can also be done by cutting joints at 45 degrees, but this technique becomes difficult to control when joints do not meet at 45 degrees.

30. The completed piece is installed over foam core wing walls and effectively covers the exposed foam edges with a clean corner connection.

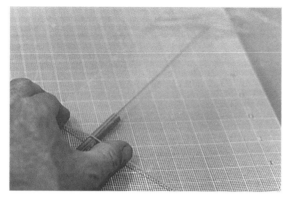

31. Plastic sheeting is cut for the window wall area by scoring it with a knife and breaking it over the handle.

32. Glazing mullion lines can be made by scoring with a knife or marked for the application of adhesive design tape.

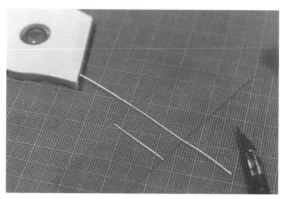

33. ⅟₃₂ in. wide white adhesive design tape is pulled across lines and trimmed to simulate 1½ in. mullions at ¼″ = 1′-0″ scale.

34. A very thin line of liquid acetate Plexiglas adhesive is applied with a knife edge.

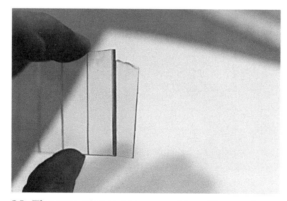

35. The two pieces are pressed together and will set, for handling purposes, in about a minute.

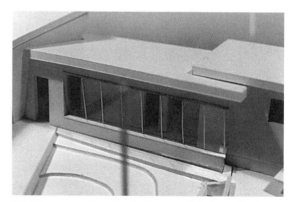

36. The completed window wall is installed in the building face.

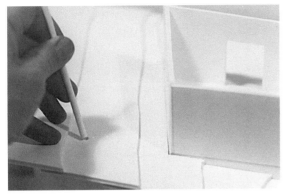

37. Large plastic rods are inserted in the site to serve as abstract trees.

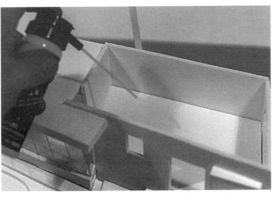

38. The model interior is cleaned out with compressed air.

39. Interior components are then built out.

40. A set of scaled stairs is inserted into the circulation tower. *Note:* ⅛ in. stacked foam core serves well as a scaled representation of ¼ in. scale tread risers at 6 in. each.

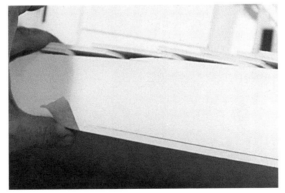

41. Finally, rough interior side supports for the contours are installed. *Note:* Drafting tape is used to draw the materials tightly together until the glue can set.

42. Finished museum board side covers are templated directly from the contours.

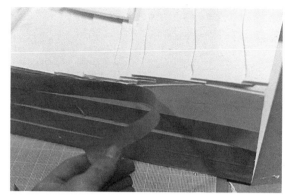

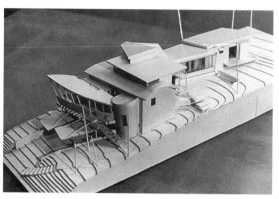

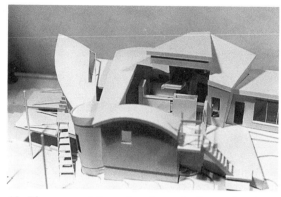

43. The sides are attached with a special adhesive transferred from a paper backing onto the material face. *Note:* Large, flat expanses of water-based glue will warp paper, spoiling the clean surfaces.

44. The sides of the model are completed. *Note:* Facing over rough cuts can convert studies to finished versions without rebuilding. See "Converting" in Chapter 3.

45. The second floor has been built so that it can be removed for a clear view of the kitchen millwork and living space. Keeping the other roofs on helps to define the interior spatial qualities.

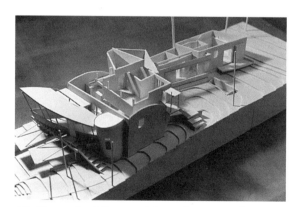

46. The rest of the model can be opened up to display various interior sections as well.

47. Construction proceeds on the project and a ½" = 1'-0" scale framing model is built in two sections (the front section is shown in the illustration) to work out all of the loading and member detailing. The model is consulted daily during the framing process.

48. The house is completed, and modeling projections can be compared.

Stage 4—Further Exploration

Strategy

The continuing possibility to serve as a site for refinement even after the building is constructed underscores the model's usefulness as an evolving site of exploration.

Assembly

This example demonstrates the use of thick, flexible acetate for curved glass surfaces.

Scale ¼" = 1'-0"

Materials

- Flexible acetate
- Plastic rods
- Museum board
- Foam core

Illustration

The presentation model is used as a further site for exploration. Three alternative approaches for enclosing the back patio area are carried out directly on the model.

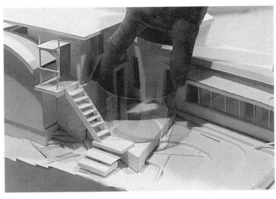

First Alternative
The finish model is used to explore porch enclosures by curving glass around slab. *Note:* Thick, flexible acrylic has been used, but the actual glass would most likely be made from tangented flat planes.

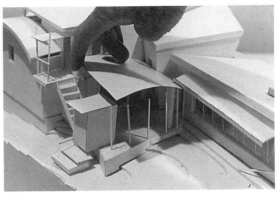

Second Alternative
This scheme explores the use of a curved roof plane with a series of columns cut from plastic rods.

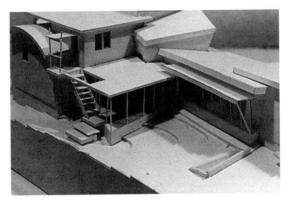

Third Alternative
A flat roof solution is tested, following the geometry of the slab below and extending out to engage the second-story stairs.

Case Study B
Multifamily Housing
Stage 1–Sketch Model

Strategy

The model is used as a drawing tool and becomes the prime generator of information.

Assembly

This example demonstrates the use of quick assembly techniques to facilitate spontaneity.

Project

Five-story, multifamily structure

Scale–not to scale

No predetermined scale is used, but the model maintains relatively proportioned relationships between its parts, such as floor-to-floor heights. These heights can be measured and assigned a scale. In this case, actual measurement the between the floors is ⅛ in., so a scale of 1″ = 100′-0″ would represent about 12 to 14 ft in height. See "Scale" in Chapter 3.

Materials

- Poster board
- Corrugated cardboard
- Chipboard

1. A linear organization is used to begin exploring the project. The model base is then punctured with a knife to provide sockets for a row of balsa stick columns. *Note:* Corrugated cardboard, with the top layer of paper removed, is used for surface texture.

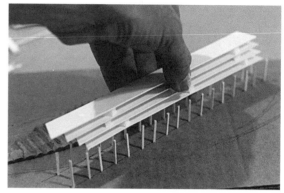

2. Columns are installed, and a stack of floor plates are mounted on top. *Note:* Floor plates have been separated by small pieces of foam core to establish equal floor-to-floor heights.

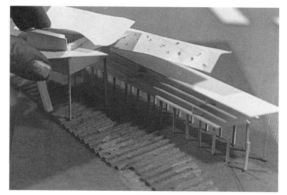

3. Using the initial framework as a focal point to visualize possible moves, roof and building body components are quickly cut with scissors and assembled. The optimum design fit for the unit is found by holding it up to various locations on the framework.

4. A contrasting vertical element is desired. Scrap metal is brought into the ensemble and is programmatically folded in as vertical circulation. The entire model took less than an hour to generate and offers many implications for development.

- Balsa sticks
- Metal fragments

Illustration

The designer constructs a sketch model with a specific project program and site in mind.

Case Study C
Sculpture Foundry
Stage 2–Development Model

Strategy

The project begins with a development model that is then translated into a small, simple finish model and illustrates the evolutionary development process.

Project

A sculpture foundry with classrooms (addition to existing facility)

Assembly

The building of multiple frames is demonstrated, and hot glue is used for attaching balsa sticks to speed the process.

Scale ⅛″ = 1′-0″

The scale is relatively large for an initial study, but is needed so that the designer can study framing members as they collide with roof components. It also provides sufficient atrium space and wall area for elevation studies. *Note:* This scale is too large in terms

of design details at this level of development and makes the model appear ungainly.

Materials

- Corrugated cardboard
- Chipboard
- Balsa sticks

Illustration

The model was initiated from scaled drawings that facilitated a direct move to the development model.

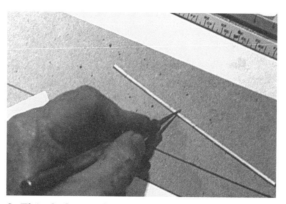

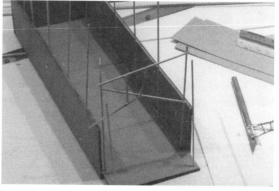

1. Following rough sketches for truss design, sticks are quickly assembled with hot glue. Time-consuming joinery is reserved for the finish model. *Note:* Measurements for additional sticks are templated directly from the model.

2. Thin balsa sticks are quickly cut by bearing down with a knife and trimming with scissors. *Note:* The model saw and miter box can be used for thicker sticks, and the ends can be sanded if a higher level of finish is desired.

3. A prototype truss is installed, along with a series of frame uprights on the model base.

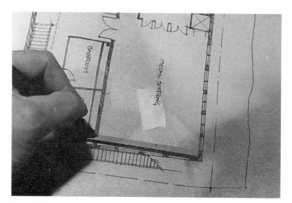

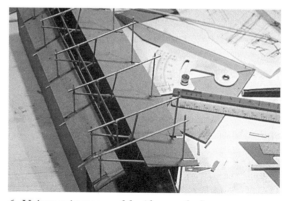

4. Trusses templated from the first construction are added. Uprights are leveled with a small triangle. *Note:* The sides serve as temporary supports and will be cut away from uprights to try alternate facades.

5. Other components, such as walls and roofs, can be templated directly from the drawings in a similar manner to the trusses.

6. Using scissors and knife, roof planes are rough cut and fitted around the truss system.

7. Smaller elements are installed and trimmed as desired once their effect on the model has been evaluated.

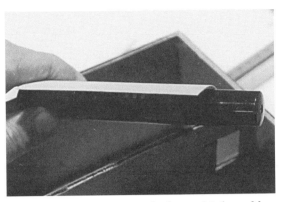

8. A curved canopy is made from chipboard by rolling the board over a felt marker.

9. Changes to openings are cut directly on the model by drafting guide lines and using a small triangle to keep knife cuts straight. *Note:* When using plastic straightedges, angle the knife slightly away from the edge to avoid cuts in the plastic.

10. An initial facade is designed and evaluated in place.

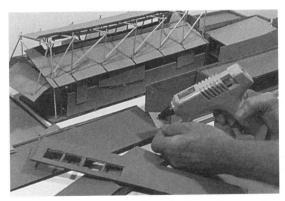

11. The wall is removed, and alternative treatments are quickly cut and glued in place.

12. To complete the investigation, a third alternative facade using overlapping planes is tested and work on the finish model is begun. See Case Study C, Stage 2.

Stage 3–Finish Model

Project

A sculpture foundry and classrooms (addition to existing facility)

Assembly

The model demonstrates assembly techniques for small plastic rods as well as the building of context and site.

Scale 1/16″ = 1′-0″

A small scale is selected to accommodate the site context and the minimal detailing of the larger model. *Note:* Typically, models increase in scale as more is known. In this case, by reducing the scale the abbreviated resolution of components becomes more convincing.

Materials

- White two-ply museum board
- White plastic sticks

Illustration

The finish model is constructed both to confirm design decisions and to present to clients without the distractions of the rough assemblage.

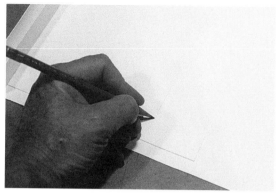

1. Drawing information is transferred with the knife to the model base, and additional lines are drafted directly on it as required.

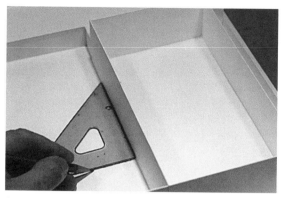

2. Lines are checked for squareness as the model proceeds and adjusted to fit the emerging construction. *Note:* Bluelines become slightly stretched when printed, and, if not checked, transferred construction lines may result in poorly fitting details.

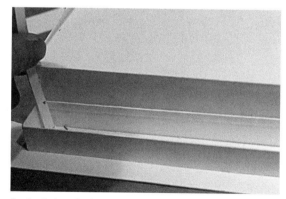

3. A gluing ledger is installed on the interior wall of the building. *Note:* The roof beyond is already showing signs of sagging because of the thin, overspanned material. The installation of reinforcing strips under the roof could have avoided this problem.

4. A knife is used to handle delicate parts.

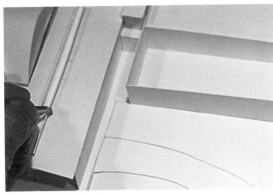

5. The flat roof tops are placed below the wall edges. *Note:* Tweezers can help in handling small pieces.

6. The initial mass model is completed, and the truss frame is detailed with thin white plastic modeling sticks. *Note:* The accepted convention is to locate flat roofs below wall edges so the resulting parapets can be read on the model.

7. Small plastic sticks can be cut by pressing down on a knife. Larger sticks and rods must be scored and broken or sawed. Ends can be sanded to a clean square finish.

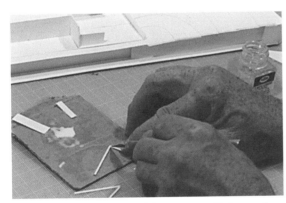

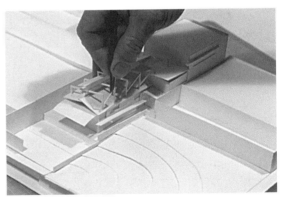

8. Plastic is joined by placing a small drop of solvent on the joint with a knife tip. *Note:* It is helpful to apply glue over a surface that will not adhere to the material, such as plastic food wrap.

9. Truss components are glued to the paper with white glue.

10. Subsequent components are installed.

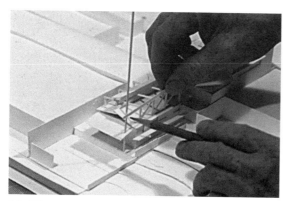

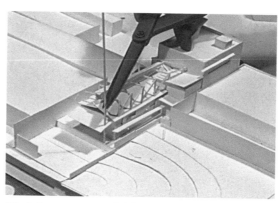

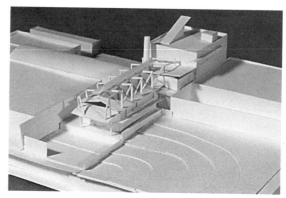

11. The exact lengths of additional components are measured directly from the model.

12. Scissors are useful for trimming pieces, as their pincer motion can be less disruptive to delicate constructions.

13. The small finish model, when side lit for contrasting shadows, can convey a surprisingly rich level of information.

Case Study D
Office Building
Stages 1 and 2–Sketch and Development Model

Strategy

The sketch model can be used in concert with basic scaled drawings to visualize a general design direction. Once the basic building begins to emerge, the model can be used as a focal point to help visualize additional moves.

Assembly

This example demonstrates techniques for constructing multiple floors and glass walls.

Project

A five-story office building

Materials

- Poster board
- Plastic sheet for glass (*Note:* For small models, thick acetate can be used, but it is not ridgid enough to be convincing at larger scales.

Scale ¹/₃₂″ = 1′-0″

A small scale is selected to reduce the building size for initial sketch studies.

Illustration

The model was generated using scaled schematic plans and sketches, and the basic construction was then used to visualize refinements to the design.

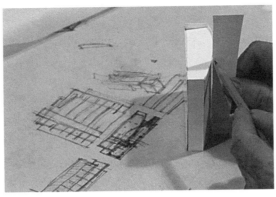

1. Scaled plan and section sketches are measured to produce initial model information. Curved pieces and other components are measured directly from the model to fit the construction. *Note:* Hot glue has been used in places for speed.

2. A drafted floor plate is attached to cardboard using a light coating of Spray Mount, and lines are transferred with a knife. The paper plans are then removed. *Note:* Spray Mount should be applied in a ventilated area.

3. Additional plates are traced from the original plate to keep cuts uniform.

4. Column centers are marked on stacked floor plates and gang drilled. *Note:* Two columns have been pierced through all four floors to hold them in place. Straight pins can be used for the same purpose.

5. Columns are passed through the floor plates. *Note:* Notches in the circulation shaft have been cut to receive the floor lines.

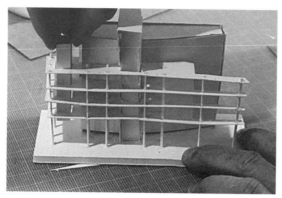

6. Plates are raised their respective levels and inserted into the shaft slots. *Note:* Connection points are premarked on the columns. The completed unit is attached to the building body, and additional shaft elements are inserted through the floors.

7. Thin Plexiglas sheets are cut for atrium glass and covered with white art tape for mullion designs. A small steel triangle is used for scoring acetate with a knife. Plastic sheeting can be broken along scored lines. *Note:* Avoid thin acetate.

8. Plexiglas is assembled using an applicator brush.

9. The partial Plexiglas construction is fitted to the body of the building.

10. The model is used to visualize terminating roof elements.

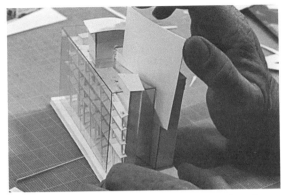

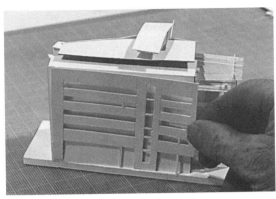

11. The Plexiglas construction is completed, and areas about to be enclosed are refaced with museum board to give the model a finished appearance. Selective parts can be recut as needed; however, refacing is generally less disruptive.

12. Window openings are cut in an overlay sheet and applied to the building face. This method is more practical than attempting to cut holes through the existing model.

13. Understated shadow lines generally read better on small models. *Note:* Additional facings can be cut and applied over all the original cuts to continue elevating the model's finish. See "Converting" in Chapter 3.

Case Study E
Urban Park
Stages 2 and 3–Development and Finish Model

Strategy

Starting with a schematic drawing to determine general plan relationships, the model is used to develop the design. At each phase, areas to be developed are based on reactions to the emerging structure.

Assembly

The project demonstrates the speed that can be attained using wood sticks, even with a dense forest of members. It also illustrates the building of base and context models.

Project

Proposal for an urban park construction

Scale 1/32″ = 1′-0″

The scale is relatively small to accommodate the large size of the site.

Materials

- Balsa modeling sticks
- Foam core and chipboard

Illustration

The model of an urban park structure, occupying a city block in length, is used simultaneously as a sketch model, development model, and finish model to develop the project.

1. As in previous examples, the model is started by drilling a series of holes in the base to install column lines.

2. The base is made from an acoustical ceiling tile. Streets are painted flat black, and concrete islands and walks are made from chipboard.

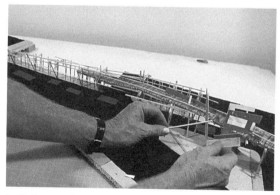

3. Balsa sticks are quickly assembled with hot glue. A concrete tower made from chipboard is integrated into this milieu.

4. Hot glue and pins are employed to keep the explorative aspects of the model moving at a steady pace.

5. Additional components are brought into the evolving design and sized in response to the other elements. Interaction between the model and the components it suggests illustrates the idea of ongoing discovery in the design process.

6. A ramp, kiosks, benches, and other program components are installed. Roof shards are cut from balsa sheets and pinned to the column/beam structure.

7. Final roof elements are added to complete the installation, and context buildings are built for the base. *Note:* Context models are built from foam core and painted flat gray with auto primer.

8. The model has been photographed at street level to convey the experience of inhabiting the space. *Note:* Curving roof forms have been made from mylar drafting film.

9. A comparison of this bird's-eye view with the previous vantage point illustrates the range of readings that can be extracted from the model with the aid of a camera. See "Model Photography" in Chapter 7.

ADVANCE
Creating Curvilinear Forms and Special Techniques

The majority of modeling materials, such as boards and sticks, are conducive to building orthogonal planar shapes. Designs may often be steered by the propensity of these materials towards planar solutions when something more sculptural is desired.

In response to some of the limitations of these materials, this chapter presents a range of techniques for making sculptural shapes. Because sculptural elements are more often needed as components of a model, many of the examples present ideas for creating individual shapes. These can be expanded to entire models if desired.

119

Equipment and Materials

Equipment

Most of the equipment used for making sculptural shapes is similar to that used for other types of model making; however, there are several specialized tools that can be helpful in working with alternative materials like wood, wire, metal sheets, and clay.

Aside from the power tools needed for woodworking, most of these tools are relatively inexpensive. For more information on woodworking and metal equipment, See "Alternative Media" in Chapter 7.

Materials

Sculptural forms can be crafted from a variety of materials. In the case of platonic solids such as cones and spheres, conventional cardboard materials or metal sheets work well. For irregular and curvilinear forms, materials such as wood, foam, clay, wire, and plaster are better suited to the task. For additional information on working with wood, metal, and plastic, see "Alternative Media" in Chapter 7.

Cutting Thin Metal Sheets

- Wire side cutters
- Tin snips
- Scissors
- Matte knife

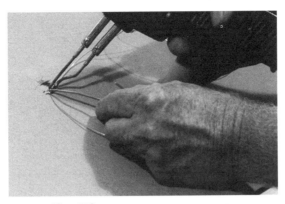

Connecting Wire

- Soldering irons (see "Basic Equipment" in Chapter 1 for soldering instructions).
- Hot glue gun
- Thread

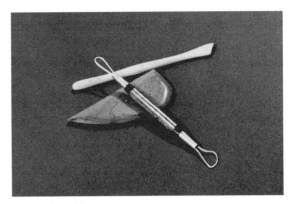

Sculpting Clays

- Cutting wires
- Shaping stick
- Smoothing board

Cutting, Drilling, Shaping

- Band saw
- Table saw
- Jigsaw
- Belt sander

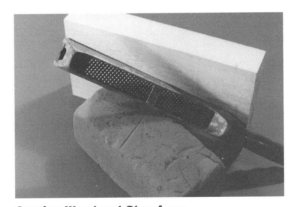

Carving Wood and Styrofoam

- SURFORM
- Hot wire

Carving Wood

- Carving knives
- Sandpaper

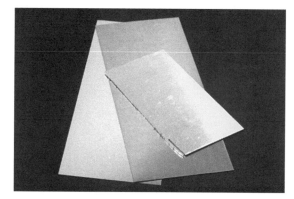

Sheet Materials

- Cardboard and paper boards
- Chipboard
- Bronze and aluminum modeling sheets

Wood Modeling Sheets

- Balsa
- Plywood
- Basswood

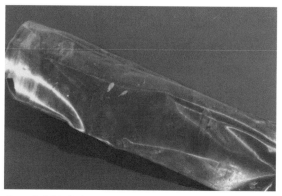

Special Metal

- Galvanized metal sheets and ducts
- Aluminum flashing
- Malleable copper sheets

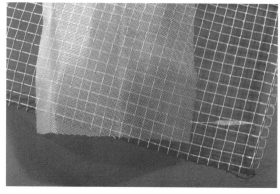

Metal Screens

- Screen wire
- Hardware cloth

Metal Rods

- Copper wire
- Aluminum wire
- Coat hangers
- Wood and plastic modeling sticks

Poured and Spread Liquids

- Molding plaster
- Papier mâché (made from white glue and newspaper)
- Perma Scene (a mâché material used by model railroad builders)

Modeling Clays

- Lizella clay
- Plasticine (plastic modeling clay)
- Sculpty (can be hard fired in a conventional cooking oven)

Cut and Carved and Shapes

- Wood blocks
- Styrofoam blocks and shapes

Found Objects

- Styrofoam and rubber balls
- Cones, drinking cups, and bowls
- Cardboard tubes
- Plastic and foam packaging forms

Found Objects

- Old tools and utensils
- Household items
- Electronic parts
- Acrylic domes

Found Objects
Modifying Objects

Many shapes, such as cones, spheres, and other complex forms, can be found in a variety of everyday objects and provide quick, accurate solutions. To match the qualities of other materials, such as paper, they may be painted or plastered. The problem in employing these materials is finding a match at the scale of the model.

Generally, found objects are not exactly the right size or shape, but by altering shapes such as cones and spheres, a large variety of secondary shapes can be generated.

Found objects can also be manipulated to integrate conventional modeling components. This may involve cutting, breaking, melting, unraveling, distorting, penetrating, and so forth, to achieve the desired integration.

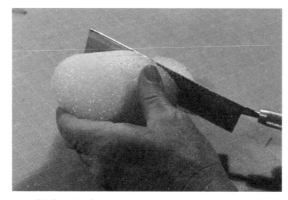

Modifying Objects
Styrofoam cones can be sawed at an angle to alter their shapes.

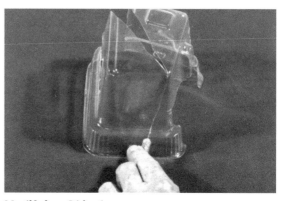

Modifying Objects
Plastic packaging can be cut with a knife to produce secondary forms.

Modifying Objects
This pasteboard cone has been truncated to change its form.

Modifying Objects
A small fragment from a light bulb is used to create a curved wall surface.

Assemblages

This model type is made with found objects and other fragments to generate ideas.

By reading or visualizing ordinary objects at another scale, the objects may be used as architectural elements. The resultant combinations can suggest forms not readily achieved with conventional materials.

Objects are most effective when used in combination with conventional model components and manipulated to yield secondary forms.

Found Cardboard Assemblage
A model using found chipboard elements. The body of the model has been cut from a cardboard dome. Sectional frames create the spherical crowning element. See "Transparent Forms" in Chapter 5.

Found Object Assemblage
Found objects and common modeling materials such as plastic rods have been combined to produce this quick assembly. *Note:* Forms such as the spray paint cap have been cut to integrate elements.

Stone Assemblage
By assembling several configurations from fragments, interesting relationships can be uncovered that other materials may not suggest.

Stone Assemblage
Not only can the fragments provide a ready collection of forms, but their material qualities convey a sense of weight not found in paper board constructions.

Metal and Plaster Assemblage
A variety of objects, including metal balls, rods, and a cast plaster site, have been used to create this assemblage.

Planar Forms

Curved Planes

Many curved shapes can be made by using common paperboard materials, as well as wood and metal; see "Alternative Media" in Chapter 7. These can be assembled as complex planar forms or used to cut patterns for curvilinear solids.

The projects on the right employ simple curved planes. Cardboard planes can be curved by rolling them over curved objects, as discussed in Chapter 2. Techniques for curving metal sheets are shown on the following page.

Curving Chipboard
The components of this sculptural model have been made from chipboard sheets.

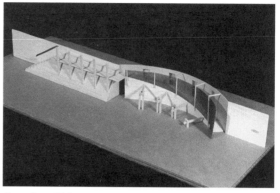

Curving Thin Wood
Balsa sheets can be used for curved sections on small models. Gluing the sheet to a base or intersecting edge can help hold the curve. *Note:* For thick wood, cutting a series of lines on the back side will allow it to curve.

Curved Metal Plane and Sphere
A curved sheet of thin metal forms the large wall. The metal sphere on top was built from pattern-cut segments. *Note:* Tape covers the joints between the segments. See "Curvilinear Solids"—"Pattern cut geometric solids" in Chapter 5.

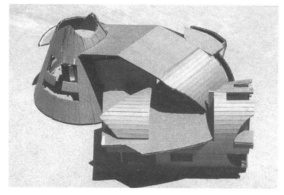

Curving Corrugated Board
To achieve a smooth curve, the board should be cut at about ⅛ in. intervals through the top layer. *Note:* The lines on the cone shape radiate from a center.

Curving Thick Foam Core
Foam core can be rolled like thinner materials, or a number of lines can be cut through the top layer of paper. *Note:* With Artcore, a layer of paper can be removed from one side.

Cutting Metal

Sheet metal can be cut with tin snips or metal stud shears. It can be cut from a variety of materials including metal ducts (shown), aluminum flashing, and copper and bronze sheets.

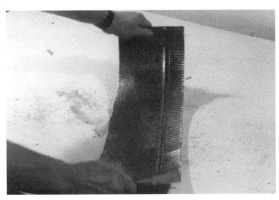

Unbending Curved Metal

Sheets cut from metal ducts can be relaxed to the proper curvature by opening the metal up and pushing out to bend it in the opposite direction.

Bending Metal Sheets

Small pieces of thin, flat metal can be curved by holding the edges and pressing with the thumbs. The sheet will have to be overbent slightly to hold the desired curve when released.

Bending Metal Sheets

Sheets can be rolled over large objects, such as this gallon paint can, to introduce curves in the same way cardboard is curved.

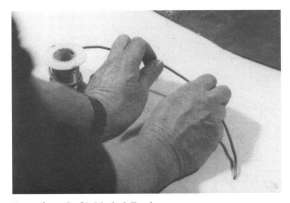

Bending Soft Metal Rods

Small copper rods and lead solder can be bent to smooth radiuses by using the thumbs and pushing outward. For longer pieces, sections can be bent incrementally by moving down the wire one section at a time.

Bending Heavier-Gauge Metal

Rods and strap metal can be bent 90 degrees in a vise by hammering at the fold line. To curve the rod, keep the vise loose and bend with hand or a hammer depending on the material thickness while continuing to pull the rod slowly through the vise.

Planar Solids

Platonic Planar Solids

Rectangles and Pyramids

Simple platonic volumes can be cut from solid blocks of wood (shown below) or made by joining flat planes. One of the most common shaped volumes in architectural modeling is found in a hip roof.

The following steps detail some of the points to be noted in constructing a simple hip roof form.

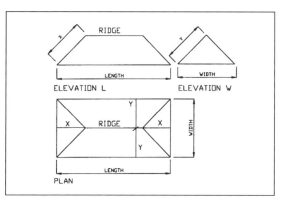

1. Elevation and plan drawings must be made to obtain true plan dimensions for the four face components. To determine plan dimension X, use X dimension on elevation L. To determine plan dimension Y, use Y dimension on elevation W.

2. Cuts should be angled inward to achieve a mitered edge. If this is not done, the material thickness of all but the thinnest sheets will collide at the joints.

Wood Massing Model

The volumes for this model have been cut on a table saw. This method can be much faster than forming the volumes with cardboard planes. The blocks can be sanded to upgrade the finish when desired.

3. The small triangular face on the right of the illustration (being put in place) has not been undercut with an angle. In comparison to the tight fit of the same element on the opposite side, this joint illustrates the potential for rough, unresolved edges.

4. Pins are used to hold the balsa sheets for assembly.

Complex Planar Solids

A large variety of planar forms can be made by attaching flat planes to define a space. Several examples are shown, using planes in a variety of ways.

Planar Solids
An endless variety of volumes and forms can be made using the relatively low technology of chipboard planes.

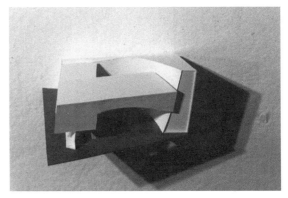

Planar Solids
Chipboard planes have been used to model these forms. *Note:* The planes have been made to warp as they follow curved surfaces.

A Sketch Assemblage
Complex forms can be sketched with chipboard planes to imply volume.

Faceted Mylar Forms
Curved and faceted planes can be used to define complex curvilinear spaces.

Basswood Mass Model
Shapes have been cut on a table saw and band saw to produce multifaceted volumes.

Transparent Forms
Exterior Skeletal Frames

These models are similar to wire frame drawings; however, whereas the "wire frame" employs a minimum amount of members to describe only the edge conditions, the "skeletal frame" incorporates a sufficient quantity of members to describe the surface of the form.

These models can describe complex forms with relative ease and have the advantage of allowing the viewer to see through to the interior space.

TWO APPROACHES TO FRAMES

1. Create a series of frames or lines, using individual members.

2. Bend and warp hardware cloth, screen wire, or other malleable sheet material.

Chipboard Frames
By cutting successive frame segments from chipboard, a curving form can be described through the visual connection of their repetitive outlines.

Warped Hardware Cloth
The model has been constructed using layers of hardware cloth bent in various configurations to define spatial volumes.

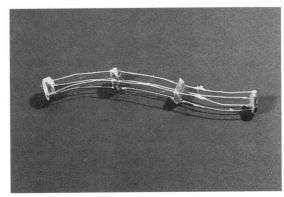

Shape Using Templated Frames
A sketch model form was made from aluminum wire and wood disks with notches cut into them to anchor the wire. *Note:* Aluminum wire cannot be soldered, so connections must be tied or glued.

Frames and Planes
A solid/void model that uses repetitive frames to describe its surfaces in combination with solid planes.

Warped Plane
Wire has been soldered in a series of ribs to describe the surface of this form.

Covering Frames

Skeletal frames can be covered with different materials to achieve the appearance of solid forms. This technique often offers the most controlled method for modeling complex curved shapes. Techniques related to this idea can be seen in the following section on working with plaster in regards to covering malleable screen wire.

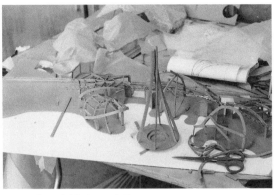

Covering Chipboard Frames
A variety of shapes can be made from strips of chipboard and covered with lightweight tracing paper.

Screen Wire Volumes
Screen wire is dense enough to read as a surface and malleable enough that it can be folded to create volumes. Screen wire may require a heavier-gauge wire frame to keep it in place.

Covering Frames
By covering a frame with material that can follow its curving surface, such as cloth, drawing trace, or mylar, solid surfaces can be created to contrast with open components.

Covering Chipboard Frames
The form has been covered with a premixed papier mâché material sold in craft stores as "Perma Scene." Tracing paper is used as a base surface. Papier mâché can also be used over screen wire and hardware cloth.

Covering Frames
Elastic stocking material was stretched over a series of frames and varnished to produce this form.

Interior Skeletal Frames

Transparent "wire frames," which outline the edges of space like three dimensional drawings, may be built to understand interior relationships between intersecting geometries. The spaces at collision points would normally be obscured by exterior wall surfaces, but because only the edges are built, overlapping spaces can be seen and developed.

To give definition to the space, it is helpful to build out all solid surfaces, such as the floor plates, that will not obscure the area of study.

Inexpensive and easily manipulated plastic drinking straws are used for this study. The straws work well as they can span large distances and can be cut with scissors and connected with Scotch tape. Other inexpensive materials to be considered are cardboard strips for curved lines and balsa sticks for large spans.

½ in. House Entry Study
This ½" = 1"-0" scale drinking straw model was built to develop overlapping interior spaces at the entry.

Transparent Mixed Media
Materials such as hardware cloth and screen wire may also be used to allow visual access for interior development.

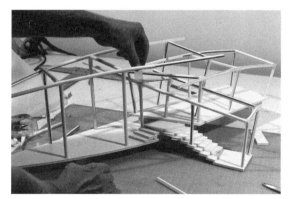

½ in. House Entry Study
By looking through the model and focusing on the edges of the three-dimensional "drawing," it is possible to visualize the relationship between the intersecting planes of the interior projection at the entry stairs.

Transparent Plastic

It is sometimes desirable to incorporate thicker pieces of plastic in models for transparent layers and bases. These materials offer similar advantages to skeletal frames in allowing the viewer to see through to interior spaces and can also be used to build visually interactive layers.

In all but the thinnest sheets, transparent plastic usually means Plexiglas. Plastic and acetate sheets for glazing (addressed in earlier chapters) are related to these thicker sheets but do not require special equipment to fabricate.

Material

Plexiglas is available in clear and colored 4′ × 8′ sheets. Thicknesses can be as little as ⅟₁₆ in. and progress to ⅛ in., ¼ in., and ½ in. Many suppliers sell scrap sheets that can be used if smaller pieces are required.

Equipment

Plexiglas sheets of approximately ⅟₁₆ in. can be cut with scoring knives or tools and broken similarly to thin plastic sheets. Thicker sheets require power tools like those used in working with wood. For more information, see "Plastic and Foam" in Chapter 7.

Plexiglas Massing Model
Multilayered colored and clear Plexiglas sheets have been cut on a band saw. The planes can be spaced with wood blocks, threaded on wood dowels, or suspended with wire.

Transparent Plastic Model
The roof form and walls employ transparent layers of plastic to reveal inner spaces and create visual interaction between the layers.

Plexiglas Walls
This model for a site space employs ¼ in. Plexiglas, etched on the surface to simulate glazing and stitched together with wire cross members.

Curvilinear Solids

Pattern-Cut Geometric Solids

Geometric or "platonic" solids such as the sphere and the cone can be made from assembled sheet patterns. The advantage to constructing them this way is that, unlike found objects, they can be made to fit exact scales.

The resulting spherical forms will be slightly flattened, as true spherical segments are curved in two directions; however, the results will be acceptable for spheres with diameters up to about 4 in.

Sphere Pattern

A sphere is made by dividing the desired volume into a series of segments, similar those described by longitude and latitude lines on a globe. About 24 segments are needed to create an acceptably even pattern. More segments can be used, but at some point they may become too small to handle. If fewer segments are used, the sphere will start to appear flattened at the sides.

Techniques used to assemble the segments are shown on the following page.

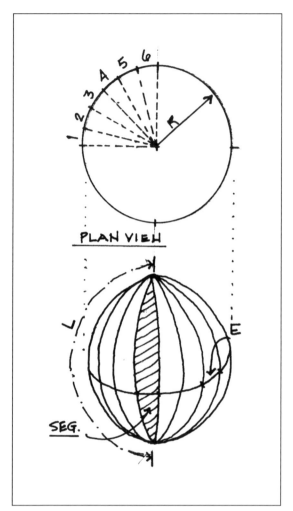

PLAN VIEW

SEG.

Conceptual View of Segment (SEG.)

Dimension E = circumference (2π R) divided by the number of segments.

Dimension L = half the circumference (length along one segment line from axis pole to axis pole).

The plan view at the top shows the layout of six segments in one quarter of the circle.

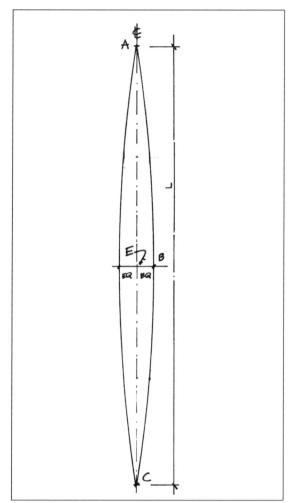

Layout for One Segment

1. Draw a center line equal to dimension L.

2. Cross the center line with marks equal to dimension E.

3. Draw a three-point arc through points A, B, and C.

Note: The sides of the segments must be curved as shown to fill space at the edges. Simple triangular shapes will not work.

Sphere Model

With the drawings used as a guide, a sphere is built from a series of curved planar segments. The second drawing is used to determine the correct size and edge radius for each segment, which depend on the desired scale of the sphere.

The process begins by cutting a series of flat segments and then proceeds by gluing the edges together to form a sphere.

1. The pattern has been cut, leaving a small section attached but scored at the middle to facilitate assembly.

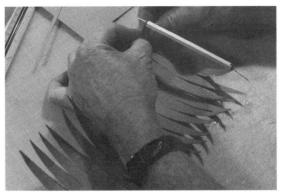

2. A stick is pinned in the middle to establish the correct diameter of the sphere.

3. Each segment is glued to the edge of the segment next to it. It is helpful to add reinforcing glue to the inside of these joints once they have set.

4. The completed sphere can be painted or covered in plaster and sanded smooth for a finished appearance.

5. The shape can also be distorted to create other related forms, such as elongated "football" shapes.

Cone Pattern

Cones can be constructed as a measured pattern or rolled from paper to quickly approximate the desired size and shape.

The construction of a measured cone is shown on the right. A rough cone assembly is demonstrated at the far right.

To produce a measured cone shape, the pattern shown below should be followed.

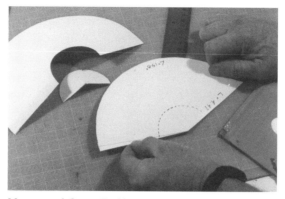

Measured Cone Pattern

A pattern cut from posterboard to form a cone with a 2 in. radius (dimension L) and 4 in. height (dimension H). The angle between L radius legs is 158 degrees. *Note:* An extra tab has been glued to the edge to join the seams.

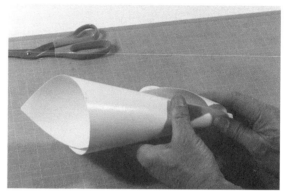

Rough Cone

To make a rough cone, material can be rolled tightly at one end and glued together.

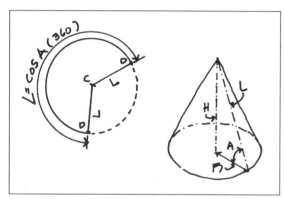

Measured Cone Pattern

L = square root of dimension $H^2 + R^2$.

To find angle A, use H/R = tan A.

The pattern will be the smaller part of the pie with the dashed line along the curve.

To Build the Cone

1. Draw two lines (L and L) from a single point, joining at the angle shown (cos A (360)).

2. Measure out on lines to find L and draw a circle from this radius.

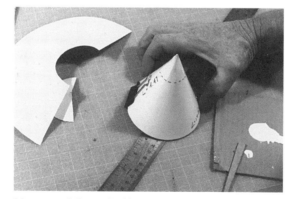

Measured Cone Pattern

The cone has been joined at the seam, using a clamp until the glue dries. A second cone may be cut from the top to truncate the form, as shown by the dashed line around the top of the cone.

Rough Cone

To trim, a circle template can be passed over the cone, traced, and cut as desired. For angle cuts, slant the template and trace around the cone.

Cut and Carved Forms

For quick assemblages, wood blocks and Styrofoam can be cut on a table saw or a band saw to provide a large range of shapes. Polystyrene foam can also be cut using a hot wire cutter.

Scrap lumber from construction sites works well for this type of assemblage and is relatively inexpensive.

For more on equipment and wood types, see "Alternative Media" in Chapter 7.

Shapes Cut on a Band Saw

Shaped forms can be easily cut on a band saw from blocks of wood. The saw can be used to do rough carving as done by a knife, but much more quickly.

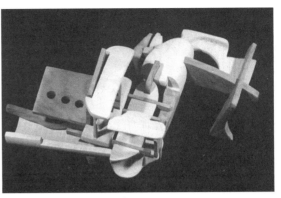

Carved and Sanded Wood

Given time, wood can be cut, sanded, and carved to make any shape imaginable.

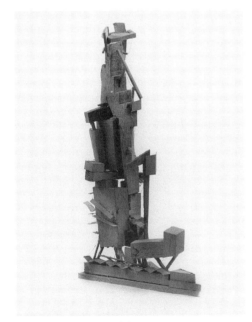

High-Rise Assemblage

A model for a high-rise tower built from band sawed wood, balsa sticks, and chipboard.

Styrofoam

Blocks can be carved with saws or SURFORMs and sanded into shapes. They can also be covered with plaster. *Note:* Use fine, even-celled blocks such as those sold for modeling or used for flower arrangement bases.

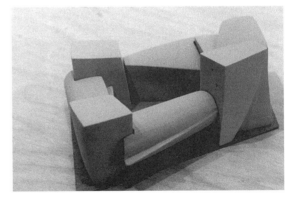

Carved Styrofoam Shapes

This Styrofoam massing model has been carved from polystyrene foam with a hot wire cutter, then sanded smooth for a high level of finish.

Cutting and Carving Wood

A variety of affordable hand and power tools can be used to cut and finish wood model parts. The following illustrations give some suggestions as to how each can be used to shape and cut wood blocks. *Note:* Although power drills are not shown, they are useful for a variety of tasks and can be used in a manner similar to the examples shown in "Cutting Materials" cutting/drilling holes, Chapter 2 and "Case Study D," Chapter 4.

Carving Wood

Shapes can be carved from blocks before or after basic shapes have been rough cut with power tools. Small hobby chisels can be used, but professional wood carving chisels will make the job go much faster.

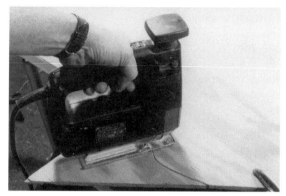

Cutting Curves

Curves can be cut in plywood and other boards with an inexpensive jigsaw. These saws are limited to wood about ¾ in. thick. Thin metal can also be cut by using metal-cutting blades.

Cutting Curves

Using a band saw is the quickest way to produce rough shapes before carving and sanding. The bed can be angled for compound curves.

Sanding Blocks

Wood blocks may be smoothed with a belt sander using 100 grit belts. Shapes can be carved using coarse belts. In many applications, shaping wood on a sander may be more effective than using carving chisels.

Cutting Blocks

Wood blocks can be quickly ripped from larger pieces of wood on a table saw. *Note:* Always use a push stick, as shown, instead of your hand when working close to the blade.

Building with Plaster

Molding plaster is a versatile material that can be used to make a variety of shapes. It is inexpensive, sets rapidly, and can be sanded to a smooth finish.

Several methods are available:

- Making forms and covering them
- Covering existing shapes
- Pouring into molds

See "Alternative Media" in Chapter 7 for mixing information. *Note:* Building with plaster can be extremely messy and is best done over a disposable surface.

The following examples demonstrate the making of curvilinear forms by covering screen wire shapes with plaster and a pre-coated casting gauze.

1. Screen wire is cut with scissors, molded into the desired form, and held in place with pieces of wire and string. *Note:* Materials such as hardware cloth can be used for armatures, but it is helpful to cover them with screen for plaster application.

2. The wire is then stuffed with newspaper to help prevent the plaster from falling directly through the screen. *Note:* This step may be omitted if falling plaster is not a problem.

3. A thin mix of plaster is made, and newspaper strips are dipped into the plaster and draped over the form. The plaster usually must be applied to one side at a time, allowing it to set before rolling the form over and coating the opposite side.

4. After the paper layer is finished and has set, a thicker batch is mixed and the paper is coated with a layer of pure plaster. When cured, this layer can be sanded smooth. Any remaining pockets or gaps can be filled with additional plaster and sanded smooth.

Building with Precoated Plaster Cloth (Rigid Wrap)

Typically, precoated plaster cloth is used to make casts for broken bones. This product, which can usually be found at craft or medical supply stores, is much easier to control than conventional plaster. A common brand of this cloth sold in craft stores is *Rigid Wrap*.

The initial smoothness of this product and the lack of waste, as compared with traditional plaster, should be evident from the example.

1. Plaster-coated gauze is used to cover a screen form by cutting strips from the roll and dipping them in water.

2. The gauze backing eliminates the need to back up the screen with paper. By crossing directions with additional layers of material, the form can achieve much greater strength.

3. After the finished form is allowed to set, a final layer of pure plaster can be smoothed over the surface to fill rough areas. When fully cured, this coating can be sanded to an even finish.

Covering Styrofoam

Styrofoam is often coated with plaster to disguise its porous surface and match paper modeling materials such as museum board. Once the plaster has set, it can be sanded smooth.

A Styrofoam ball is covered with plaster and sanded smooth.

Plaster-Covered Ball
1. A layer of plaster is spread over the ball. Often this must be done on one side first. After this side has set, the other side can be coated.

Plaster-Covered Bowl
This half-oval shape has been covered with a thin coat of plaster. *Note:* The shape was carved from a block of Styrofoam.

Plaster-Covered Ball
2. The ball is sanded smooth. Plaster tends to clog up sandpaper, and of several fresh sheets will be required for final smoothing.

A Plaster Surface
This warped plane was made by stretching screen wire over a wire frame and covering it with plaster. *Note:* Gauze was used instead of newspaper to carry the plaster.

Coating Chipboard

Existing shapes can be covered with a layer of plaster for texture or to match white paper. Spackling or premixed sheet rock finishing compound can be used for this purpose as well. Integral color can be achieved by mixing a small amount of powered dye with the plaster or spackling. Chipboard is used as a base because it allows the plaster to grip its relatively porous surface. Although it offers the simplest form of backing surface, this material is not ideal. The water content inherent in plaster can cause it to lose its form, and the surface grip is such that plaster may flake off when dried. These problems can be partially solved by using heavier material and reinforcement and gluing cloth to the surface to provide extra gripping power.

Spreading Plaster on Chipboard
Plaster can be spread directly onto chipboard and sanded smooth. Several layers may be required to achieve the desired consistency.

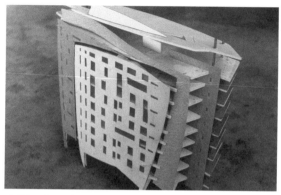

A Plastered Model Facade
The surface of this building facade has been covered with spackling to produce a textured finish. *Note:* Integral color has been used on one of the layers to provide contrast.

Plaster Contours
Although contours can be covered with plaster, a negative mold of the site can also be made and cast in plaster. See "Molding with Plaster and Resins" in Chapter 5.

Plaster Contours
Contours of this site model have been built up by applying spackling over chipboard and sanding it smooth.

Molding with Plaster and Resins

Plaster can be poured into molds to form a variety of shapes. Pouring plaster is particularly advantageous in making multiples of the same form and for pouring monolithic (solid) curved shapes.

The molds are constructed as the negative of the desired form. This method is similar to forming techniques for cast concrete, and concrete formwork manuals are full of ideas.

The processes that have been discussed to this point have been additive in nature; that is, the shapes and forms are built up by attaching pieces. The molding process is different from this, because before an object can be formed, its opposite or "negative" must be constructed.

Plaster must then be poured into the form, or negative, to yield a "positive" shape. Forms can be poured as solids or backed with cloth to create "thin shell" forms.

The following projects were made using casting techniques. Basic casting and mold making techniques are illustrated in more detail on the following pages.

Multiple Forms

The multiple forms for this multistory study were made using a wire frame mold. Successive pours were popped from the mold and strung together on the three columns.

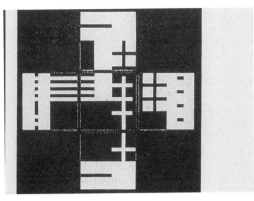

Plaster Cast Model

A form was made to translate the four faces of this figure ground drawing into negative space and make a mold for the plaster casting below.

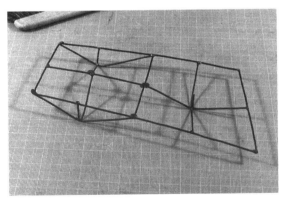

Molding Frame

This frame was covered in tape and used to create the plaster mold for the example above. *Note:* The mold was greased with petroleum jelly to keep the plaster from sticking. Pam (cooking spray) can also be used.

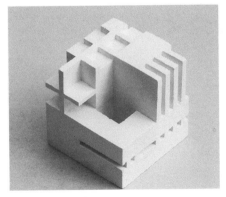

Plaster Casting

Wood and cardboard solids were placed inside a box-shaped form to leave the negative space in this casting.

Basic Casting

Casting plaster and other materials involves the use of a mold or negative. This form will be the reverse volume or "negative" of the form you are trying to make. For example, if the desired form is a half sphere, the mold will be a bowl.

To remove the casting, the mold must be flexible or slightly conical. If sides are "undercut" or have a lot of texture, the casting may be caught in the mold. Undercuts can be employed if the mold can be peeled away or broken off. A release agent is needed to help keep the material from sticking to the mold. A thin coating of petroleum jelly can be wiped on the form or cooking oil in an aerosol can can be lightly sprayed on the form.

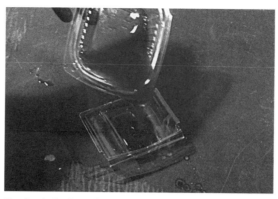

Project A–Pouring Resin
Following product mixing directions, polyester resin has been combined with a catalyst and poured into a plastic mold that can be peeled off. Common release agents cannot be used, as they will react with the resin.

Project A–Cast Resin and Mold
The mold is peeled from the hard resin casting. Resin offers a very smooth surface finish. It can also be bought as a clear casting resin at craft stores. *Note:* Dyes of various colors can be added to clear resin as desired.

Project B–Pouring the Mold
Plaster has been poured into a muffin pan sprayed with a release agent. This mold is ideal, as the sides are slightly conical. If the sides sloped in the opposite direction, the casting could not be extracted.

Project B–Reinforcing the Casting
Wires or sticks can be pushed into the wet plaster to reinforce the casting. These act like the steel rods in reinforced concrete, supplying tensile strength to the material.

Project B–Casting and Negative Mold
After about 30 minutes, the plaster can be pulled from the mold. *Note:* The "positive" form of the plaster is the opposite of the "negative" form of the mold.

Casting Molds

Casting molds or "negatives" can be made from a variety of materials. They do not have to be elaborate constructions. All that is required is that they hold the plaster until it is set in the desired shape.

The examples on this page show a number of possibilities. Some of these methods are employed for simplicity, such as the cardboard box technique, and some are used to allow undercuts.

Cardboard Box Mold

Boxes can be used as molds by lining the corners and cracks with duct tape. The mold can be torn away from the casting and discarded.

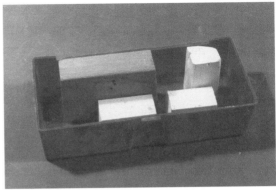

Rubber Box or Bucket Mold

Rubber boxes and buckets work well because they are flexible and can be expanded to release a casting. *Note:* Objects have been placed in this box and will leave spaces in the casting wherever they displace material.

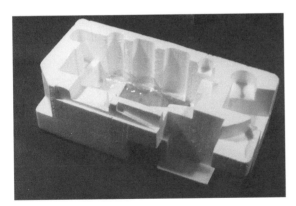

Found Object Mold

Interesting mold shapes, or "negatives," can be found in packing spacers and other found objects. The shapes that would result from pouring this mold must be visualized by reversing the image of the negative volume.

Plastic Mold

Clear plastic molding material can be bought or found as a variety of packaging items. This molding material can be peeled away from the casting, allowing the use of limited "undercuts."

Casting in a Wood Box Mold

A wood box may be built by nailing sides to a base board or holding the sides with weights as shown. All of the objects higher than the sides of the box will become holes through the casting. *Note:* A release was sprayed on.

Augmented Casting Methods

Postcasting Techniques

After the initial pour, operations such as the casting of additional layers or pushing objects into wet plaster can be used to further manipulate the casting.

Form Removal

Several techniques may be used to break the casting from the mold and extract objects from the plaster.

The casting of additional layers is illustrated at the top of the page. Problems of form removal are demonstrated below.

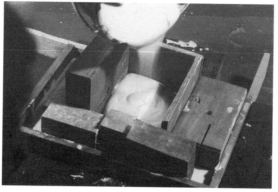

Building Up Casting
Using the casting shown in fig. 5.114, another set of forms is built on top to add layers to the pour.

Imprinting Forms
The formwork has been removed to reveal the built-up section as well as the depressions made by pressing blocks into the wet surface of the casting.

Removing Objects
Cardboard and plastic forms can be pulled away easily from a dry casting. Other objects can be extracted only once the plaster is trimmed back with a knife. Gluing objects to the base will help stop plaster leaks.

Removing Objects
The use of clay or Plasticine allows some undercutting to be employed, but these objects must be dug out of the casting. If wood blocks are used, they should be sanded and slightly tapered or they will not come out.

Negative Cavities
The holes were created where plastic film containers were taken out of the casting. *Note:* The casting will be fragile for some time after it is set and is easily broken with the stress of removing objects even after curing.

Malleable Materials

Malleable materials such as Lizella clay and Plasticine can be easily formed to take on complex sculptural shapes. Of the two materials, Plasticine is generally used because it does not dry out and crack. In addition, because it is not water based, it can be used in combination with paper materials.

It can be difficult to achieve hard edges with malleable materials, and they often require internal wire and wood supports to maintain their shape. However, there is no need to build a negative form (as required in casting plaster models), and subtracting parts is relatively easy.

Clay is worked with sculpting tools such as cutting loops and shaping sticks, kitchen knives, and smoothing boards. See "Equipment" earlier in this chapter.

For forms that will set hard after molding by hand, materials such as "Sculpey," a ceramic hybrid available at craft stores, can be molded and fired in an ordinary kitchen oven.

1. Modeling material has been cut off a block of Plasticine and formed by hand. Material can be removed as desired with a kitchen knife and sculpting tools. *Note:* The material is easier to work when it is warm. Hand molding will help transfer body heat.

2. Wire loops like those used for working with clay can also be helpful for carving out recesses in the material.

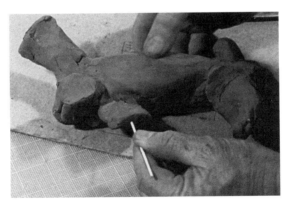

3. Cantilever projections can be supported by inserting wire or wood rods through these sections into the body of the model.

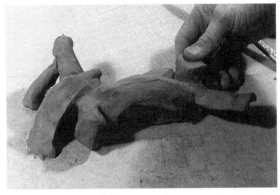

4. The completed form can be smoothed out by hand or with sculpting tools. *Note:* Removal of all hand marks can involve an inordinate amount of time.

Malleable Site Model

A Plasticine site model can be molded in a similar manner to the actual site soil and used for quick studies. *Note:* It can be difficult to transfer final grade elevations from this type of site model.

Plasticine Free Forms

The plastic possibilities for complex curving forms made from Plasticine are limitless.

Clay Free Form

Traditional clay can also be used to create any plastic form, as in this sculptural composition.

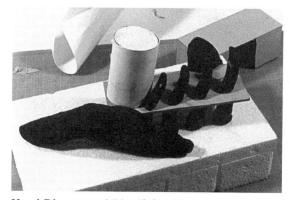

Hard Planes and Plasticine Model

Shapes such as the repetitive conical "finger" forms can be effectively modeled from Plasticine and combined with planar sheets to create the hard-edge elements.

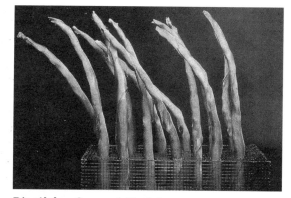

Plasticine Concept Model

This spatial interpretation of the book *Everglades: River of Grass,* by Marjory Stoneman Douglas, is facilitated by the plastic qualities of clay materials.

Multimedia

Although the models presented in earlier chapters have generally been made using one type of material, various materials can be combined to make a model. This has already been seen to some degree in contrasting site materials as well as in glazing and screen wall applications. Further use of multimedia can help establish the coding of elements, as discussed in Chapter 3 "Development: Coding and Hierarchy of Materials," and also helps convey a sense of materials as they relate to the project's meaning and finishes.

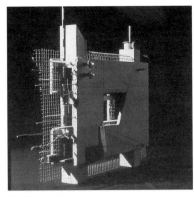

Multimedia
A simple two-part combination of heavy wood planes and light wire hardware cloth helps to reinforce the binary dialogue of the project.

Multimedia
A collection of materials, including foam core, chipboard, wood, and cork sheeting, materials helps to code each section of the model to create a readily understood ensemble.

Multimedia
A large model measuring 4 ft in height, this construct employs Plexiglas, steel, and plaster to convey the dynamics of the space and the materiality of the primary elements.

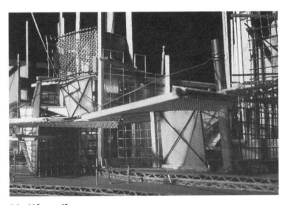

Multimedia
A combination of wire, hardware cloth, paper, foam core, and wood sticks has been used; these are materials that readily lend themselves to modeling elements such as columns, planes, and open grids.

Multimedia
A concept model using wood shards and sticks with foam core and Plasticine (curving lines in center). Materials have been selected based on contrasting colors and their ability to form shapes and planes.

BUILD

Implementing Model
Exploration as Built Work

Examples of model usage can be found at every level of the design environment, ranging from sole practitioners to firms with international reputations. In practice, modeling offers one of the strongest ways to understand the impact of design decisions on the built work and is of particular value in working with complex geometries.

The following projects present examples of models from several types of practices. Many of the strategies discussed in Chapters 3 and 4 can be seen at work, as well as the connection between built work and the model history that helped form it.

Scogin, Elam and Bray Architects Inc.

This leading design firm makes extensive use of the model in the development of every project. A cross section of work reveals many of the strategies discussed in Chapter 3 applied in response to a particular need or situation. Whereas the structure of one project may be difficult to understand without the aid of a detail model, another project may require a scaled-up section to study the spatial experience.

The role of the model is also seen to vary, depending on the way the design evolved. In some cases a combination of models and drawings has been used, and in others, multiple alternates or exclusive reliance on the model formed the rule.

Examples drawn from six different projects are used to illustrate the diverse role of the model in the daily course of this firm's practice.

Buckhead Library

Atlanta, Georgia

The models from the project demonstrate two primary ways they are treated. First, because the project was initially developed with the drawings, a small ⅛″ = 1′-0″ scale model was built to confirm decisions. In the second instance, in order to develop the entry sequence and canopy elements, the front section was increased in size to a ¼″ = 1′-0″ scale. At this scale the model was large

enough to convey the experience of moving through the space. The image of the completed building confirms the ability of the scaled-up model to predict a reality.

Buckhead Library–⅛ Scale
This small development/finish model was made after the overall design relationships were established and depicts a three-dimensional sketch of the entry canopies at the front of the building.

Buckhead Library–¼″ = 1′-0″ Section
The front section of the building has been doubled in scale in order to develop the design of the entry canopies. The model and elevation drawings were used in concert to compose its elements.

Buckhead Library–Completed Building
The completed building, in a view similar to that taken of the ¼ in. scale model, reflects the quality of space the model projected in early studies.

BIS Competition

Berne, Switzerland

Laban Dance Centre Competition

Deptford Creek, London, England

Reston Museum

Reston, Virginia

Models played a central role in the development of these three projects. The models used for the Reston Museum demonstrate a strong reliance on alternatives. In the BIS competition, the idea of alternatives was expanded to the production of numerous parts, combined to create dozens of schemes. The Laban Dance Centre models were generated in an extensive progression.

BIS Addition–Scheme 1
This project required three schemes for an addition to the central conical tower. A small context model of the urban area was used to test relationships with the urban context.

Laban Dance Centre–Full Model Array
The full evolutionary array of models used to develop the Laban Dance Centre design are shown and include every possible stage of development with many alternate explorations.

Reston Museum–Alternative Schemes
Five alternatives were developed for this project. After using drawings to help develop the program on the first model, small 2-D sketches were used to initiate the other schemes.

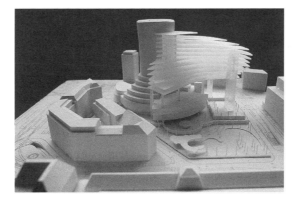

BIS Addition–Scheme 2
In the course of developing schemes, numbers of alternative variations were generated. In this view the addition takes the form of a series of shifted layers rotating off the tower's axis.

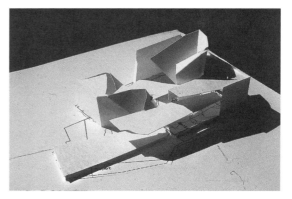

Laban Dance Centre–Sketch Model
A small sketch model extracted from the model progression at the point where early conceptual models were first translated into program space.

Morrow Library
Morrow, Georgia

Beginning with a small concept drawing, most of the design work was carried out directly in model form. Three clear stages of model progression were used, along with a scaled-up model of the central tower.

Unique to the project was the construction of an adjustable model to test roof relationships, as well as the production of construction drawings from measurements taken from the models. To produce drawings of the tower shown below, the model was not only measured but photocopied and traced to create elevations. See "Transferring Model Data" in Chapter 7.

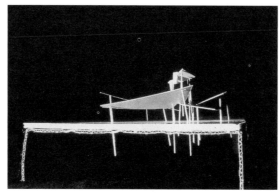

Morrow Library–Adjustable Model
The model was constructed to operate like a puppet and used to adjust relationships between the roof planes. The corner points of each roof could be moved by pulling sticks protruding below the baseline.

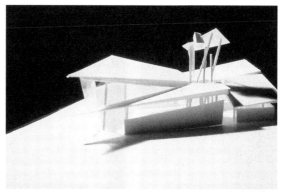

Morrow Library Development Model
Once basic relationships were established, a small study model was made to refine the general relationships. The tower model shown on the left below was made to develop its components.

Morrow Library–Finish Model
At this point the design was generally complete, and elevation drawings were made to complete the study. Exposed structure was used in the building, and the final model included all of it to study its visual effect.

Morrow Library–Completed Building
When implemented, the building confirmed many of the decisions the model helped to resolve.

Turner Center Chapel
Atlanta, Georgia

Although several of the previous examples included scaled-up sections used to work out ideas, the Turner Center Chapel project approached the need for closer study by employing a combination detailing/framing model. Owing to the close proximity of interwoven truss members, the lower half of the finish model was scaled up to a ½" = 1'-0" model and used to work out (or resolve) the detailing relationships for the glazing connections.

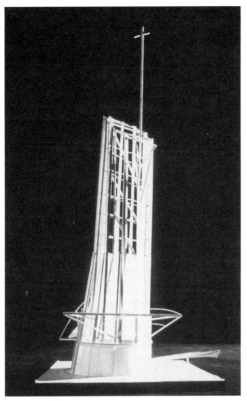

Turner Chapel—Finish Model
This model was preceded by several small model studies, and the entire structural system was drawn on the computer to precisely locate dimensions and angles. Although the 80 ft steel building to the left attests to the eventual success of the design, what could not be understood at this point was the three-dimensional interaction between steel members in the lower half of the tower.

Turner Chapel—½" = 1'-0" Model
The lower section of the tower was glazed, and a framing system that would insure against warped surfaces was required. To work out the detailing, the lower section was scaled up and each member modeled to within an inch. Although computer modeling may have been a viable alternative, two-dimensional computer drawings did not provide enough information to control the complexity of relationships. The completed tower on the far left speaks to the success of the model.

Callas, Shortridge Associates

Seagrove House (in progress)

Santa Rosa Beach, Florida

Among other projects, this firm has designed many outstanding houses and uses the study model as a site for exploration throughout the process.

The model is key element in understanding the dynamic space of the Sea Grove House. Of special interest is the evolution of model refinement, particularly in the development stage, and the use of the model on the site as a tool for construction visualization. The images on this page compare views of the on-site model and the project as it nears completion. All roofs are constructed so that they can be removed from the models to reveal interior spaces and framing systems.

Seagrove House—Finish Model
North elevation of the final model used during construction to understand overall relationships and framing. The model has been increased in scale from the last development model on the following page and detailed.

Seagrove House—Finish Model
South elevation of the final model. When compared with a similar view of the built work, it becomes clear that the model space carries strong predictive powers.

Seagrove House—Built Work
As it nears completion, the active space of the built work reflects the model's ability to orchestrate the composition. On entering, the space exceeds the promise of the model.

Seagrove House—Built Work
The built work offers two different readings from front to back. Whereas the north elevation breaks apart to perform a dance in space, this elevation engages the southern horizon.

Seagrove House

Study/Development models

These models represent explorations used to define various sections of the building. At this point, a rough general scheme has been established and study begins by orchestrating the overall building. As sections are generally resolved, focus can be seen to shift to alternate solutions for individual elements.

The study culminates in a development model with relationships similar to those of the finish model but less detailed.

Seagrove House–Stage 1

At this point the house appears related to its final form, but the walls have yet to be defined. Individual elements are only suggested, and other forms of expression are explored.

Seagrove House–Stage 2, Front

The major elements on the north elevation appear to be formed at this stage, and alternate elements such as the angled box (with taped corners on the second story) are experimented with.

Seagrove House–Stage 2, Lakeside

The south elevation of the development model appears generally formed. Study has been focused on the tower and the spaces directly below it.

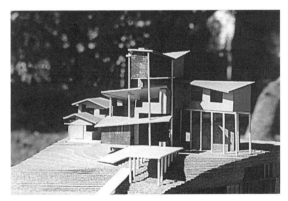

Seagrove House–Stage 3, Lakeside

At this point most of the spaces on the south elevation have been established and final refinement can take place.

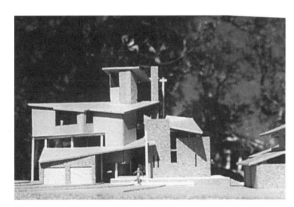

Seagrove House–Stage 3, Front

This development model is similar to the final model, except that less attention has been given to detailing openings and intersections.

Kohn Pedersen Fox and Associates PC

This well-known firm uses study models on a regular basis. Although the projects are substantially larger in size than the previous examples, models are used in a similar manner and help to convey an understanding of the overall relationships. Of particular interest in this series of illustrations is the use of multiple variations built to refine a central design direction.

US Airways Airport

Philadelphia, Pennsylvania

In the US Airways terminal project, a number of alternate forms of design expressions are shown, with the final resolution on the far left. The plan view shares many of the qualities of a figure-ground facade study. This relationship between the two-dimensional quality of facade models and plan views can be used to organize the program and expression of large, complex projects.

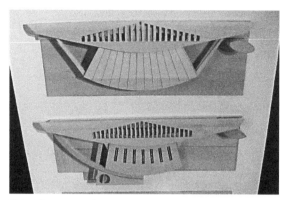

US Airways Airport
Balsa wood studies of the overall airport design, shown above and below, explore alternate roof treatments. At this level of development the overall relationships are relatively constant.

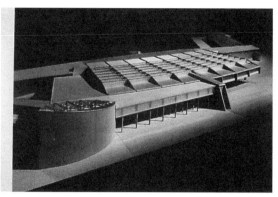

US Airways Airport
The final model has been photographed at a lower level to convey experiential and formal qualities of the space.

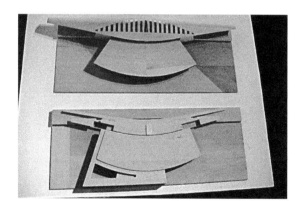

US Airways Airport
These alternates treat the main body of the terminal as closed surfaces and employ different treatments for ancillary circulation elements.

Posteel Tower
Seoul, South Korea

Dongbu Security Headquarters
Seoul, South Korea

Engineering Building
University of Wisconsin

The images on this page display a series of models made to refine projects. At this stage in the process, a scheme has been determined and multiple iterations or facade studies are carried out. Although some of the models are sized on the order of sketch models, their position in the process renders them closer to development models.

Posteel Tower
These small paper models explore a number of variations on interlocking facade elements to articulate the building as an ensemble of parts.

University of Wisconsin Engineering Building
A development/finish model built to work out and detail elements of the facade. See "Facade Models" in Chapter 1.

Posteel Tower
The models have been incrementally increased in scale as the study begins to home in on a design direction.

Dongbu Security Headquarters
Subtle changes to explore the interaction between vertical planes take place within well-defined parameters. At this point in the design process, each of these models could be considered a finish model.

Ropongi Tower

Seoul, South Korea

The models for this project illustrate the idea of increasing scale to explore greater levels of resolution. The study moves from small alternates to a series of models that are scaled up to study various sections. As the study proceeds, the overall relationships remain fixed, with each new area under study growing progressively focused.

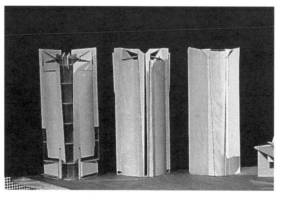

Small-Scale Alternates
The initial scheme has been established, and six small development models (three shown) are used to explore alternate treatments to the front elevation. In this sense, they could also be considered facade models.

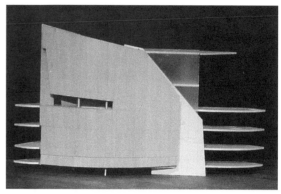

Tower Termination–Partial Segment
A section of the top of the tower has been increased in scale again to focus in on detailed studies of the design.

Ropongi Tower
The tower is increased in scale to produce a wood finish model. The six smaller studies can be partially seen to either side of the model. Three of these earlier studies are shown above.

Tower Termination Study
The central section at the top of the building has been increased in scale to refine the design exploration.

Tower Termination–Partial Segment
An alternate treatment for the tower top.

Venning Attwood and Kean Architects **161**

Venning Attwood and Kean Architects
Harvey Law Offices
Atlanta, Georgia

The nature of interior space is such that dynamic planes and elements can be extremely difficult to understand in drawing form. Although these designers typically work in model form, it was particularly important for this project that decisions be made with study models. Views of the built space are paired with model views and reveal the way the model allows the viewer to "walk through" the space.

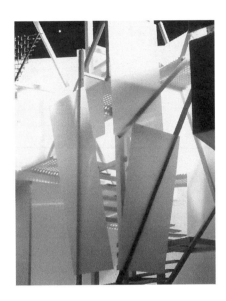

View Up Central Stairs/Law Library

The model view above left shows the screen panels and hyper space described by the stair structure. The image at the top right was taken looking into this area. The screen panels, stairway, and bookshelves can be seen moving up through the space.

View Along Entry Wall

The view of the model space to the right is taken in the hallway as one enters the space along the curving wall. The model face has been cut away to allow vision into this area. The image on the far right of the built work was taken in the same space on the opposite side of the curving wall.

MC² Architects Inc.

Hemphill House

Atlanta, Georgia

Dekalb Avenue House (In Progress)

Atlanta, Georgia

This design-build firm uses the model to great advantage on every project, which underlines the point that modeling can benefit every form of practice.

Models for the projects were used in concert with drawings to develop the houses. The projects were built as speculative intown developments and focused on aspects of the site to direct the model studies. The models are from the development stage of the projects, and although sketch model studies were made early on, many of the important issues of expression and detailing were resolved directly on these models.

The model for the Hemphill House was used in several ways, but one important aspect, illustrated above, was the framing detailing for the roof structure. The model for the Dekalb Avenue House illustrates the development of the long, sweeping granite in relation to the built work below.

Hemphill House Model
The roof structure describes a hyperbolic curve. Every member has been creatively engineered to shape the design and control its weight as it floats over a glass clerestory.

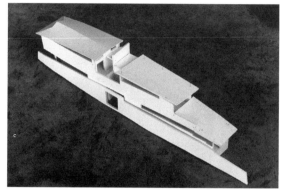

Dekalb Avenue House
The model is a good example of a solid/void study at the development stage; ultimately, it helps guide the detailing to make the building appear to rise out of the linear granite wall.

Hemphill House
Although the shallow curve is difficult to see in this small image, the flying roof form reads well as it hovers over the house below. Careful study with the model ensured that the detailing of the roof supports maintain this reading.

Dekalb Avenue House
Relationships established by the model can be seen to have been carried through in the built work as the house nears completion.

Roto Architects Inc.

This firm employs a flexible, improvisational working style that adapts to the inevitable and unique aspects of each project. Much of the work has been designed and built through collaborative relationships with clients. In the course of this collaboration, various design methods have been explored with modeling playing a key role in the development of new systems.

Sinte Gleska University

Antelope, South Dakota

Sinte Gleska University is the first and oldest tribal university in the Americas. Roto Architects was asked to plan and build an entirely new campus for the university. The project used models to develop highly refined readings of the spatial and diagrammatic structures of the Lakota traditional systems of movement and rest. The detailed model of the multipurpose building displays many of the aspects discussed in respect to focusing and hierarchy.

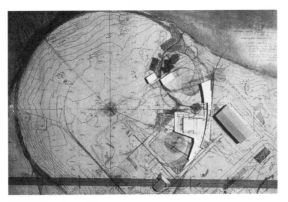

SGU Master Plan
Models and drawings have been used in concert to map out site relationships that reflect traditional Lakota spatial systems.

SGU Multipurpose Building
Modeling elements were used to develop and detail every structural member and incorporate traditional Lakote beliefs in a layering of ordering systems.

SGU Technology Building and Student Center
The ribbed roof structure, moving from left to right, employs modeling to describe the form of a mythological star formation bridging between the two buildings.

SGU Multipurpose Building
A detail of the Kapemni, or universal model (center), considers every structural element in relation to scale and hierarchy extending attention down to the 27 symbolic ribs of the buffalo as shown in the center of the roof structure.

Teiger House

Bernardsville, New Jersey

This project sought to express concepts of dynamic human organizations in three-dimensional diagrams. The models and drawings were used to develop linear, incremental ordering systems with frequencies and phasing that worked simultaneously in plan and section.

The finish model reads as a series of units that reflect this system, and the framing models reveal the incremental aspect and simultaneity of layers. This ability to see through the layers of the framing model makes it a valuable site for exploration of internal relationships, as discussed in "Transparent Forms" in Chapter 5.

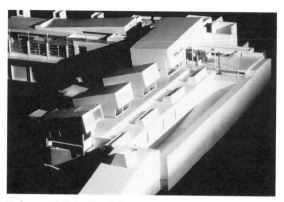

Teiger Finish Model
Although the built work employs a variety of color and materials, the model relies on abstraction to allow materials to be imagined and to convey the overall pattern of formal relationships.

Teiger Framing Model
The transparent nature of the framing model is not only used to develop sectional relationships, but plays on the conventions of the repetitive framing members to establish an incremental ordering system.

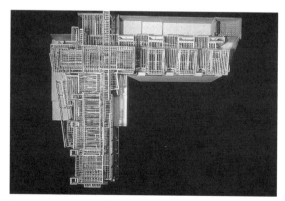

Teiger Framing Model
The overlapping rectangular frames set up multiple ordering relationships when apprehended as a stack of superimposed images.

Dorland Mountain Arts Colony

Temecula, California

This project replaces a small retreat building for an arts colony. The building reflects the way indigenous structures form unique volumes, based on the constraints of time and materials. The models are an exercise in three-dimensional drawing. By placing key members to shape the volume, a structural frame is developed that springs from unique construction and bracing systems.

Carlson-Reges Residence

Los Angeles, California

This residence was built as a series of additions grafted onto an existing industrial building. Materials were primarily brought into the project from a scrap yard adjacent to the building. As much of the work was developed as an ongoing work in progress, models were used to direct overall moves on each section and to evolve expression during construction.

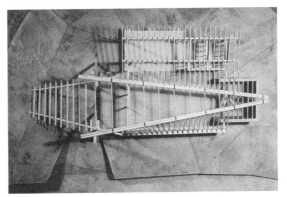

Dorland Mountain Arts Colony
The diagram of the triangulated frame and its subsystems can be clearly read in plan view.

Dorland Mountain Arts Colony
The volume generated by filling in the spaces demonstrates the effectiveness of using a 3-D diagram to establish the skeletal outline. The model also facilitates the rethinking of triangulated bracing systems.

Carlson-Reges Residence
The quality of the existing space is reflected in this interior model, and the effects of the new light monitor can be experienced just as it might read in the space. See "Interior Models" in Chapter 1.

EXPAND

Topics for Continuing Exploration

This chapter provides further information concerning alternative media, related models, transferring model dimensions, photography, computer modeling, and detailed presentation models.

Alternative Media

Most of models in this book have been made with paperboard materials. These materials are valued for being inexpensive, quick to assemble, and easy to modify. As such, they are ideal for the majority of study models; however, there are situations in which it is advantageous to use wood, metal, plastic, and plaster in model making.

These media can be combined as an expedient way to construct components or employed for expressive purposes. Although they may not completely reflect the behavior of full-scale components, they may provide a better understanding of material properties.

The use of these materials has been touched on in the previous chapter, and although a detailed treatment is beyond the scope of this book, the following sections augment earlier information on material choices and the equipment used to work with them.

Plastic and Foam

For plastic materials such as Plexiglas, the tools applicable to working with wood can be used effectively. Plexiglas can be cut with table saws or band saws, and belt sanders can be used to smooth and shape the edges. If clear, polished edges are desired, a strong electric buffing wheel is required. Grit compounds for buffing can be purchased in gradated degrees of coarseness and applied to the wheel in three applications. Starting with coarse grit compound and moving to medium and then to fine, edges and can be buffed to a clear, smooth finish.

Polystyrene is a dense foam suited to cutting and shaping to make quick sculptural forms. Blocks or sheets can be laminated together with contact cement, or with construction glue to create larger pieces. Although the material can be cut with hand or power saws and shaped with a SURFORM tool, a hot wire cutter can make shaping more accurate. The wire cutter uses a tightly strung heated wire to slice through the foam. The pieces can be guided by hand or held steady by mechanical guides similar to those found on a table saw. The foam can then be sanded to even out surface variations.

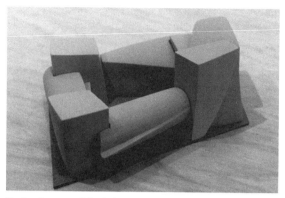

Polystyrene Model
The blocks of foam that make up this model have been cut with a hot wire and sanded smooth.

Wood

Constructions made from wood are often built as finely crafted presentation models. For this level of finish, books found in "Resources," at the end of this chapter, are good sources of information. However, for study models and simple presentation constructions, there are many uses for wood. For massing models and sculptural shapes, wood blocks can be cut quickly with a band saw and sanded smooth with a belt sander (see "Cut and Carved Forms" in Chapter 5). Balsa sheets and sticks can also be used to produce finish constructions with simple equipment, as shown to the right.

Materials

For simple models, wood sticks and soft wood scraps work well. Woods with an even grain structure and a degree of softness, such as mahogany or basswood (ironically, classed as hardwoods), are the preferred materials for high-level finish models. Many of these materials can be found at hobby or modeling supply stores; however, for larger blocks of mahogany or basswood, a hardwood lumber supplier is the most likely source. Large blocks can also be made by glue laminating smaller ones together.

DIMENSIONAL MODELING STICKS

- Balsa—inexpensive and cuts easily
- Basswood—more expensive, but holds form better than balsa and ends can be sanded with accuracy
- Mahogany—often used for rich color with similar qualities to basswood
- Oak dowels—must be sawn for clean cuts

SHEETS

- Balsa wood sheet—finished appearance, cuts easily, spans well, and reflects material thickness of smaller-to-midsized models
- Modeling plywood—similar properties to balsa; can be cut with a power saw or rough cut with a matte knife and sanded smooth

WOOD BLOCKS

- Balsa
- Basswood
- Mahogany
- Pine, spruce, cedar, fir—common softwoods used in residential construction and entirely adequate for study models

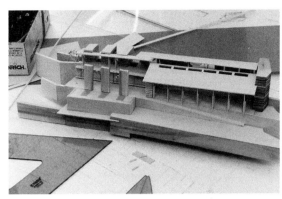

Wood Presentation Model

The planes for this model are typical of those that can be made from thin basswood sheets and modeling plywood.

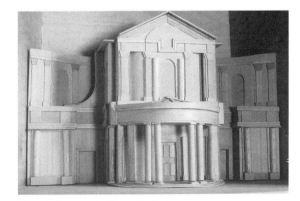

Wood Presentation Model

Components have been cut from even-grained wood blocks, using a range of power tools typically found in a wood shop. This level of craft is best suited to modeling after all design decisions have been worked out.

Woodworking Equipment

For balsa sheets and all sticks, simple X-acto knives and modeling hand saws can be used. All other wood materials (especially blocks) require power tools or carving knives.

The basic power equipment needed to work with wood includes a table saw, a band saw, and some form of belt sander. These can be inexpensive tools, as the wood is relatively soft and cuts will probably be small.

For sculptural shapes, power tools can be used to produce rough shapes. Carving tools and power sanders can be used to finish the shapes.

Table Saw

An inexpensive table saw with an 8 in. blade. On low-end saws such as this, the rip fence is inaccurate and must be checked with a square. *Note:* Avoid small modeling table saws, as they are very underpowered.

Belt Sander

Hand-held home construction types or pre-mounted units can be used for model sanding work. Shown is a hand-held type. It can be mounted with homemade clamps or with an aftermarket bracket.

Drill Press and Hand Drill

A drill press can be useful in making accurate holes. Inexpensive models will serve well. Alternately, a hand drill can be mounted on an aftermarket stand and used as a substitute until use of a drill press is warranted.

Hand-Held Jigsaw

This type of saw can be used for rough cuts and limited curved cuts. It is wise to compare the power ratings on jigsaws, as many inexpensive saws can cut only the thinnest of materials.

Band Saw

Shown is a minimally sized two-wheel saw. *Note:* Avoid inexpensive three-wheel band saws; because of tight wheel radiuses, they break blades regularly.

Metal

Models are rarely constructed entirely from metal; however, rods, wire, and shaped planes can be very useful as component pieces.

Materials

Many of these materials can be found as common items in hardware stores. Small rods and tubes, as well as sheets of aluminum and bronze, are available at most hobby and modeling shops. Heavy-gauge metal can be purchased at a metal supply yard.

THIN SHEETS

- Aluminum and galvanized flashing
- Galvanized metal
- Copper, bronze, and aluminum modeling sheets
- Screen wire—aluminum, bronze, and fiberglass
- Hardware cloth with holes from ⅛ in. to ½ in.

WIRE, RODS AND TUBES

- Copper, brass, and steel wire
- White plastic-coated wire
- Copper and brass rods and tubes
- Coat hangers
- Heavy-gauge steel and aluminum wire
- Reinforcing bars

ALUMINUM SHAPES

- Rods
- Round and square tubes
- Angles

HEAVIER-GAUGE METAL

- Rods
- Square stock
- Plate steel
- Angles

Fabrication Equipment

Connecting, cutting, and bending heavier metal parts can be involved.

Connecting

For small rods and plates, joints can be soldered or, in some cases, hot glued. For larger pieces, bolted or welded connections are required.

Welding on thin metal with arc welding equipment tends to burn holes in the metal very quickly. For best results use a small MIG welding unit (recently available at reasonable prices). These units feed a thin wire from a spool to serve as a constant welding rod and are easy to use. They are also surprisingly portable and have low power requirements. Thin metal can also be brazed with oxyacetylene torches and spot welded. *Note:* Without more specialized equipment, aluminum cannot be welded.

Cutting

For small rods and plates, hacksaws and tin snips can be used. Cutting of thicker metals, other than those for which tin snips are applicable, can sometimes be accomplished with metal-cutting abrasive wheels used in a circular saw or in an electric miter box. Metal blades in a powerful jigsaw or "Saws All" can be effective for cutting sheet metal up to 1/16 in.

For heavy cutting, equipment beyond that which is common to most model shops is required: oxyacetylene torches, power hacksaws, nibblers, metal-cutting band saws, plasma torches, and shears.

Bending

Thin sheets and wire rods can be easily curved and bent by hand. Some pieces can be held in a vise and bent with pliers or hammers. Anything thicker will require special equipment and is usually not used. However, for those interested in bending thick metal

- It is necessary to heat large solid rods with an oxyacetelyne torch before bending.
- Thick metal sheets require the use of a "bending brake."
- Structural shapes such as tubes and angles must be passed through a "rolling mill."

Plaster

Material

Molding plaster, also referred to as hydrocal, is available in small cartons at hardware stores or in 100 lb bags at Sheetrock supply stores. Be sure to specify "molding" plaster, as other varieties are prone to shrink excessively when drying.

Tools

Once plaster has cured, it can be sanded, cut, and carved similarly to wood with many of the same tools such as SURFORMs, sandpaper, carving knives, chisels, and band saws.

Mixing Plaster

For small batches, one-gallon plastic buckets, plastic containers, and cut-down milk jugs make excellent mixing bowls. For larger batches, five-gallon paint and Sheetrock buckets serve well.

Plaster is mixed in a ratio of about two parts plaster to one part water. This means that any container should start just about one-third full of water. It is helpful to leave some room in the container for adjusting the mix. Plaster is then shaken into the water in a sifting manner until an island of plaster begins to form on top of the water. At this point, the solution is mixed by hand until all lumps are smoothed out. The mix should be about the consistency of pudding or thinner for coating tasks. For papier mâché–like applications, the mix should be runny. With practice, you will be able to get the proportions right the first time, but until then, the mix can be thickened by adding plaster or thinned with more water.

The working time until plaster begins to set is about 10 to 20 minutes, so it is best to mix quickly to allow time for application. If you work fast enough, successive batches of plaster can be mixed in the same container without cleaning it out. However, once a batch has begun to harden in the container, it can no longer be used, as lumps will be carried into the new mix.

Using cold water can retard setting time, and warm water will speed it up. Plaster will set hard, if the mix is made correctly, in a matter of 30 to 40 minutes. Additional layers can be built on top of a first layer of plaster right away, but must sit for a number of hours before water has evaporated sufficiently to allow sanding.

Cleanup

Containers must be cleaned of residual plaster before reusing them. If left to dry in a flexible plastic container, plaster can be popped out. To wash containers, use a bucket of water so waste plaster can settle to the bottom of the bucket and be thrown out later. All plaster should be put in trash cans and never down the sink, as it will settle and block plumbing drains.

Conventional Molding Plaster
Very flexible, affordable, and readily available.

Precoated Plaster Cloth
Best suited for covering wire forms.

Related Models

Artwork

Models can be used for large-scale design projects, such as site or gallery installations, the same way they are used for building design. The strategies and techniques for three-dimensional exploration are completely applicable and can serve to work out ideas that otherwise may remain only partially developed.

Illustration

The examples for the two gallery installations on the right were approached in a similar manner to interior models, with all design work being conceived directly on the models.

In each case, the study model for the project is shown at the top, with the actual full-scale construction displayed below.

Without the ability to test model elements in relation to each other, full-scale visualization would have been very difficult.

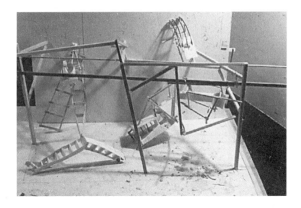

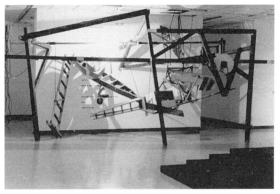

Gallery Installation

This sketch model was used to develop the frame and suspended characters for the full-scale construction below. The model was built to 1" = 1'-0" scale because of the small amount of space it represented and the need for large-scale details.

Balsa sticks, museum board, and wire make up the parts.

Sculptural Machine

The design for the "Painting Machine" shown below was worked out with a ½ in. scale model. Although many of the details were developed on the full-scale construction, all the major relationships had been investigated on the model and provided a clear map for the full-scale construction.

Transferring Model Data

Measuring Models to Locate 2-D Drawing Dimensions

Projects that have been executed completely in model form can be measured and translated to two-dimensional drawings by the following methods.

How to Measure

Points of intersection in space are measured with the scale rule as X, Y, and Z dimensions from a base plane and two 90 degree reference lines. It is helpful to buy or construct a small scale rule suited to the delicacy of the work. Make sure that the base of the ruler begins at 0'-0".

A triangle is used to mark the height of the intersection above the table plane. The triangle also helps to locate the correct point on the measuring rod directly over (normal to) the edge of the reference grid below. See the section on the Morrow Library in Chapter 6.

In complex cases (and with much larger budgets) architects may employ digital equipment similar to that used for aerospace design. A digitizer is placed at the desired points on the model, and X, Y, Z coordinate readings are automatically recorded to generate drawings.

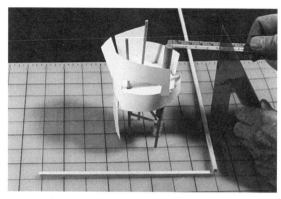

Measuring the Model
The ruler is extended 90 degrees from the reference grid to mark the X dimension of a point. The height is marked on the triangle, then the ruler is swung 90 degrees to record the Y dimension.

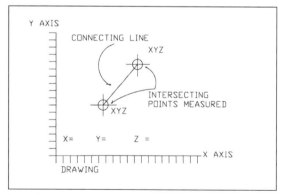

Drawing
The X, Y, Z coordinates are located on the plan drawing. Lines between the points are connected to describe the form in plan. *Note:* Z coordinates can be shown only on elevations and sections but should be noted on plans.

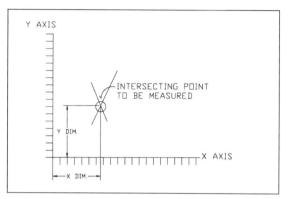

Plan View
This view is looking down on the point to be measured. The X and Y axes correspond to the sticks at the edge of the grid. The resulting X and Y dimensions would be transferred to paper and noted for their height above the plane of the measuring surface (the grided Table Top shown below).

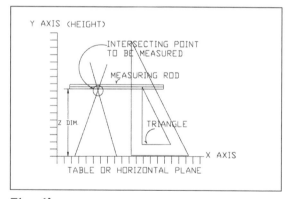

Elevation
The height (Z axis) of the point to be measured should be marked on the triangle. *Note:* The triangle also helps maintain a 90 degree relationship between the reference grid and the measuring rod.

Drawing the Model in 2-D Views

When modeling information precedes drawn information, models must be measured and converted to two-dimensional plan, section, and elevation drawings. Although this must be done in a way that will ensure accurate building dimensions, only key intersecting points are actually needed for construction.

Plotting every point needed to draw complex geometries can be a time-consuming process. Accurate numbers must be used for intersections, but shortcuts can be employed to draw reasonably accurate images of the model both for visualization purposes and to show elevation details.

Two common methods for converting models to plan and sectional drawings are shown on the right. Both of these methods involve taking 90 degree views, "normal" to the plans and elevations, with either a camera or a photocopier. See the next section, "Model Photography."

Photographing
Models can be photographed "face on" and traced from enlarged prints.

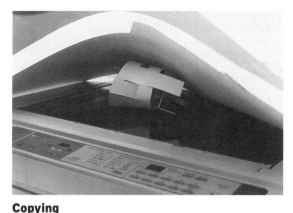

Copying
Models can be placed directly on the glass of a copying machine to make elevation images. See the Morrow Library in "Build," Chapter 6.

Photographed Plan View
The warped planes of this model are difficult to fully measure. By reducing them to a plan view, they can be drawn with a degree of accuracy and ease.

Photocopied Image
The resultant images can be traced and scaled. They will be somewhat distorted, but the directly measured X, Y, Z coordinates will ensure construction accuracy.

Model Photography
Photography Techniques

Although detailed information on film types, shutter speeds, and lens openings is limited, the following guidelines can produce acceptable results using a 35 mm camera. It is highly advisable to photograph models as soon as they are finished, as time quickly takes its toll on these constructions.

Film

Whether you are shooting indoors or outdoors, daylight print film is the most flexible and forgiving type of film. You can also use Ektachrome slide film, but the exposure tolerances will be tighter. Film speeds range from 100ASA to 400ASA. The lower the number, the more light you will need; however, the resolution is much better with 100- or 200-speed film.

Exposure

Images tend to remain focused in foreground and background areas (depth of field) at a smaller lens opening, about F8 to F16. White models can bounce so much light off of their surfaces that light meters often call for openings smaller than required. It is wise to test the meter reading with a neutral gray surface. Moreover, for the best insurance against the variables of artificial light sources, it is important to bracket your shots (take exposures above and below the meter readings).

Outdoor Lighting

Shooting outdoors is the easiest solution to lighting. The camera will tend to read lighting conditions correctly, low-speed film can be used, and automatic cameras are effective. A calm, sunny day with the sun at a lower angle in the sky (early or late in the day) produces the best modeling shadows. Experiment by turning the model around and watching through the lens as different shadows are cast.

Day Lighting
High-contrast lighting effects can be captured on very clear days with lower afternoon or morning sun angles.

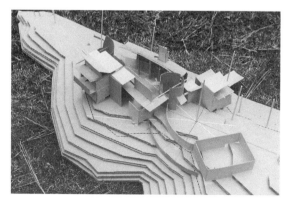

Shaded Day Lighting
Even light can be obtained in outdoor settings on overcast days or in large shaded areas.

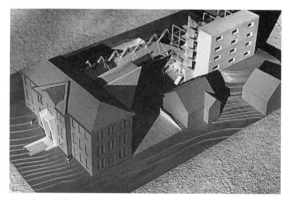

Day Lighting
The sun can be used for medium contrast as well, by avoiding extremely clear conditions and working closer to midday. Models should be turned in the sun to find optimum shadow angles.

Indoor Lighting

Lighting can be accomplished by using a single blue "photoflood" light (compatible with daylight film color characteristics). The use of a single source of light will allow you to simulate the shadow-casting effects of the sun. Light can also be bounced of a white board to soften its effects and control the way it hits the model. For even lighting, two lights can be placed on opposite sides of the model. The light source must be out of the camera eye, preferably behind it to avoid hot spots. To help with this, a hood can be used on the lens to shield side light from the lamp.

You can also photograph a model indoors, using daylight from a north-facing bank of windows, with a tripod and very slow shutter speeds. The camera can be hand held down to shutter speeds of about ⅕th second, using a steady hand or something to brace against. Shutter speeds cannot usually be controlled on automatic cameras.

Daylight Lighting
Models can be photographed indoors with sufficient daylight. North-facing clerestory windows work well to avoid unwanted mullion shadows and provide plenty of light. Slow shutter speeds are recommended.

Grazing Light on the Model
A single-source lamp can be used from below to graze light across the model. The light can be bounced off white sheets or covered with cloth to soften harsh effects.

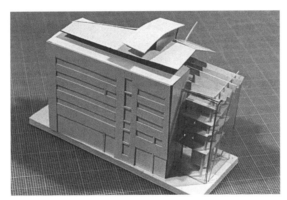

Even Lighting
Using two light sources placed slightly in front and to either side of the model provides an evenly lighted surface.

Single-Source Light
Strong shadow patterns that make the forms read as sculptural objects can be created by using a single light. For best results, turn the model and move the light to experiment with shadow angles.

Views

Models can be photographed from many angles, depending on what one wishes to communicate. Overall or bird's-eye views can convey a sense of the total building. Low views, shot up into the model, can give the effect of being on the site looking up at the building. A model scope (a special device like a small periscope that can be fitted to the camera) can be used to photograph interior views and help capture eye-level views. Special extension tubes and other lens devices can also be made to bring the camera eye down into the model more affordably.

Models can be photographed "straight on" to eliminate as much perspective as possible and create images similar to elevation drawings. These views can be useful as tracing guides to produce orthographic drawings from models, as discussed in the preceding section, "Transferring Model Data."

The sculptural or modeled view is probably the most common one used for capturing the overall geometry of a model as a three-dimensional object.

At Eye Level
An eye-level view is taken at a height of a scaled figure to simulate the view of a person moving through the space.

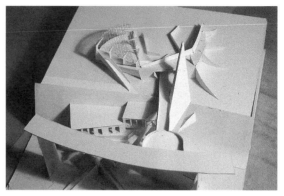

Bird's-Eye View
A bird's-eye view is taken looking down on the model and provides an overall picture of a complex or an object.

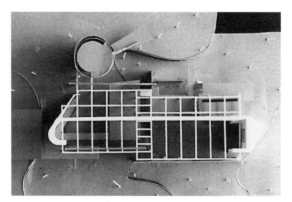

Plan/Elevation View
This view is a frontal shot taken 90 degrees to the model plane. Images of this type simulate orthogonal drawing views and can be used to convert model views to plan drawings by tracing over them.

Sculptural View
A sculptural view is similar to a bird's-eye view, but taken from lower angles to display the three-dimensional quality of the forms.

Backgrounds

A smooth, regular-textured background with some tonal contrast to the model, such as chipboard, black cloth or brown kraft paper, can work well. Clean, even surfaces such as concrete or carpet can serve as backgrounds out-of-doors, as long as there is enough area to keep the edges out of the camera frame.

Several ideas are shown to illustrate how backgrounds can work, ranging from the natural sky to gray backdrop paper.

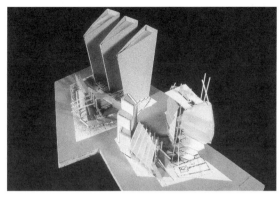

Black Contrasting Backdrop

For light-colored models, dark backdrops such as black cloth or backdrop paper can be used to highlight tones. For dark models, light paper can be used.

Blue Paper

The outdoor sky can be easily simulated with blue paper placed behind the model.

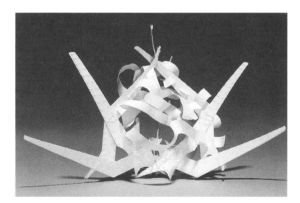

Curved Backdrop

Although dark backdrop paper or cloth can completely negate the background, gray or white paper, placed under the model and rolled up the wall will create a smooth gradation of tones.

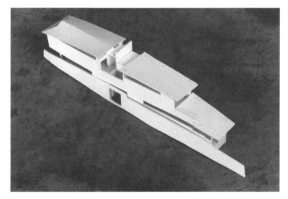

Natural Even Surface

A concrete floor, sidewalk, carpet, or other even-toned surface can be used as a neutral background. Light surfaces should be sought for dark models and dark ones for light constructions.

Natural Sky

The outdoor sky can be used by placing the model on a ledge and shooting into the model at an angle that will crop out all other background objects. This works best facing north in order to avoid glare from the sun.

Computer Modeling
Modeling Programs

The ultimate aim of any design aid is to provide valuable information in an efficient manner. Although a case has been made for the advantages of building physical models, computer modeling can also provide very useful information and should be investigated for its potential advantages. The following observations and resources can help in selecting appropriate software.

The speed and sophistication of computer modeling have increased rapidly over the last decade, but debate persists over its ability to match the intuitive nature of physical modeling. Moreover, because of the extrusional logic used by most programs, XYZ coordinate points must be used to create diagonals and warped planes and can be cumbersome as compared with the directness of angling cardboard planes. This limitation is compensated for by the ease with which forms can be manipulated. In addition, inherently common operations for a computer, such as duplication, distortion, and overlay, can become powerful tools for discovery.

Although facility can be developed to the point where drawing speed on the computer will compare favorably with that of physical modeling, the chief advantage of these programs lies in their ability to render a model and produce construction documents after the model has been developed. By cutting

horizontal and vertical sections through the model, plans, elevations, and sections can be instantly established to begin two-dimensional (2-D) construction drawings. To render the model, surfaces can be colored and a sun angle selected for shading effects.

To implement construction documents and rendering effects, a different set of software is required in addition to the modeling program. To make production drawings from a three-dimensional (3-D) model, a graphics software set is required. To render the model, rendering software or a "rendering engine" is needed. Most of the widely used programs come with 2-D graphics software and 3-D modeling software bundled together. Usually, compatible rendering software is available for these programs as a separately purchased item. Any modeling program under consideration should employ what is referred to as "solid modeling." This means that the forms it generates will appear as solids instead of "wire frames" and when cut or manipulated will present solid surfaces. By simulating the way physical models behave, solid modeling allows computer-generated models to be manipulated with greater intuitive ease.

Another aspect that should be considered in shopping for software is the ability to translate modeling information between different software packages. Although many companies claim compatibility with other software, even the smallest problems with translation can render this capability useless.

For this reason, many designers prefer to use software with all three drawing components (modeling, 2-D graphics, and rendering applications) from a single source. However, there are programs that are stronger in certain areas of application than others, and it may make sense to use some of these individually if they can be successfully integrated into your other software. To allow the user to make an initial test for compatibility, many companies offer sample software that can be downloaded from the World Wide Web.

Although the operation of the these programs is beyond the scope of this book, a list of some of the most popular software is offered as a beginning guide. Most, if not all of these programs, are available for PCs (Windows) and Macintosh platforms and all employ solid modeling.

Software Guide

Although the software industry is changing so rapidly that any recommendation stands a chance of being outmoded in less than a year, the following is offered as a current guide to programs. The first three programs are listed primarily for their modeling capabilities. Of these, Form Z seems to be the first choice of many designers owing to its ease of operation and intuitive "physical model" characteristics. MiniCad and GraphiSoft have also been well received, and MiniCad is often recommended for its competitive pricing. If purchase of the following relatively expensive software is out of reach, MiniCad could be a good alternative.

Company: Auto. Des. Sys
Modeling program: Form Z
Rendering engine: Render Zone

Company: DIEHL Graphsoft
Modeling program: MiniCad

Company: Graphisoft
Modeling program: ArchiCad

The following two programs (AutoCad and MicroStation) have become standards in the industry for production graphics. Because they include well-developed modeling capabilities and can be enhanced with rendering software, they are often selected for compatibility. In this case, the issue of compatibility goes beyond internal integration, as their use also ensures compatibility between all members of an architectural/engineering design team.

Company: Auto Desk
Modeling program and rendering engine:
AutoCad 12, 13, and 14, 3-D Studio

Company: Bently
Modeling program and rendering engine:
MicroStation TriForma

For further research, see the book and article listed below.

Stephen Jacobs. *The CAD Design Studio: 3D Modeling as Fundamental Design Skill.* New York: McGraw-Hill, 1991.

Steven S. Ross. "Entering the Third Dimension." *Architectural Record* (June 1998): 175–180.

Resources
Presentation Models

Highly detailed presentation models are usually built after design work is completed and can make only limited contributions to the design process. However, there are times, such as at elaborate client or marketing presentations, when detailed material simulation is called for. The following books offer information concerning these types of presentation models.

Rolfe Janke. *Architectural Models.* New York: Prager, 1968.

Wolfgang Knoll and Martin Hechinger. *Architectural Models/Construction Techniques.* New York: McGraw-Hill, 1992.

Akiko Busch. *The Art of the Architectural Model.* New York: Design Press, 1991.

Supply Sources

Most of the basic modeling supplies can be purchased at local art supply stores or campus bookstores. If stores are not available in your area, several chain stores sell through the mail. Two well-known stores are Charrette and Dick Blick.

Charrette
31 Olympia Avenue
Box 4010
Woburn, MA 01888-9820
1-800-367-3729
E-mail Custserv@charrette.com

Dick Blick Art Materials
P.O. Box 1267
695 US Highway 150 East
Galesburg, IL 61402
1-800-447-8192

Many of the materials used in model making can be found in hobby shops and hardware stores, including, lichen and model trees, wood and plastic sticks, balsa, basswood sheets, modeling plywood, metal rods, bronze and aluminum modeling sheets, small metal parts, sandpaper, molding plaster, Perma Scene, and spray paint.

Plastic sheets for windows can be found at Plexiglas suppliers. Thin plastic cover sheets on inexpensive picture frames carried by variety and drug stores can also be used. For very thin window material, sheets of acetate can be purchased at art supply stores and are usually available in several degrees of thickness.

Some of the more specialized drafting and cutting equipment such as Acu Arcs, can be found at architectural printing companies and through Charrette.

Common wood such as such as pine, spruce, and plywood can purchased at building supply stores.

Blocks of hardwood such as basswood, poplar, and mahogany can be found at hardwood building suppliers.

Although a range of metal components such as aluminum tubes and angle iron can be found at well-stocked hardware stores, steel supply yards will be the most likely source for square stock, steel rods, and heavy-gauge sheets.

Sheet metal suppliers that stock metal ductwork, flashing, and gutter materials can be good sources for rolls of copper and galvanized sheets.

Large quantities of molding plaster in 90 lb bags can be found at drywall supply houses.

The following people have contributed models and built work to this book and are credited for their contribution to the diversity and strength of its contents.

Academic Architecture Programs

Clemson University, College of Architecture, Arts and Humanities

Studio Critic: Criss Mills

Third year design: *Gabriella Bumgartner*–page 57, top right, bottom right. *Rene Binder*–page 68, top right, bottom right.

Florida International University, School of Architecture

Studio Critic: Rene Gonzalez

Design 1: *Amparo Vollert*–page 14, top right. *Marcus Centurion*–page 26, top left; page 148, bottom middle. *Angel Suarez*–page 58, top right, bottom right. *Desmond Gelman*–page 70, top left, bottom left.

Design 3: *Maria Pellot*–page 14, bottom right. *Mauricio Del Valle*–page 73, top left, bottom left.

Design 7: *Mark Marine*–page 14, top left; page 73, top middle, bottom middle. *David Boira*–page 26, bottom left.

Georgia Institute of Technology, College of Architecture

Studio Critic: Bruce Lonnman

First year design: page 13, top right; page 19; bottom left; page 25, bottom right. *Josh Andrews*–page 12, bottom right; page 55, top right, bottom right. *John Sitton*–page 17, bottom right; page 128, bottom left; page 177, bottom right. *Trent Hunter*–page 60, top left, bottom left.

Studio Critic: Lee Kean

Second year design: *Greg Sugano*–page 13, bottom right; page 73, top right, bottom right. *Brian Karlowitz*–page 131, top left, bottom middle.

Studio Critic: Tahar Messadi

Third year design: *Fauzia Sadiq*–page 82, top right; page 85, top left, top right, bottom left, bottom middle, bottom right. *Micah Hall*–page 14, bottom left.

Studio Critic: Harris Dimitropoulos

Mike Piper–page 20, bottom left; page 49, bottom left; page 60, top right, bottom right; page 63, bottom left; page 75, top left, bottom left; page 178, bottom right. *Casper Voogt*–page 66, top left. *Bernard Gingras*–page 66, bottom left. *Jason Van Nest*–page 129, bottom left, bottom middle. *Sam Hoang*–page 177, top right.

Studio Critic: Denise Dumais

Fourth year design: *Cameron Beasley*–page 20, top left; page 80, top middle, bottom middle.

Studio Critic: Michael Gamble

Graduate design studio: *Rob Bartlett*–page 15, bottom right; page 168, top right. *Tim*

Black–page 20, top right. *Meridith Colon*–page 63, top left. *Daniel Maas*–page 142, bottom left. *Jason Vetne*–page 169, top right.

Studio Critic: Chris Jarrett

Graduate design studio: *Lyle Woodall*–page 79, top right. *Garvin Smith*–page 63, bottom right. *David Guirdry*–page 80, top right; page 149, top left.

Studio Critic: Charles Rudolph

Graduate design studio: *Troy Stenlez*–page 13, top left; page 19, bottom right; page 60, top middle; page 66, top right, bottom right; page 87, top left, top right, bottom left, bottom middle, bottom right; page 177, top left. *Daniel Maas*–page 23, top left. *Howard Chen*–page 18, bottom right.

Studio Critics: Charles Rudolph and George Epolito

High school career discovery class: page 25, bottom left; page 179, top right.

Iowa State University, Architecture Department

Studio Critic: Karen Bermann

Pre-Architecture Studio: *Michelle Swanson*–page 57, top left, bottom left. *Brian Lee*–page 58, top left, bottom left. *Kate Podany*–page 71, top right, bottom right; page 179, bottom left. *Jim Hosek, Mike Grace, Kip cox, Stephanie Clay*–page 68, bottom middle. *Amy Skinner*–page 72, top middle, bottom left, bottom middle. *Lindsey Bresser,*

Melissa Myers, Jason Kohler, Nick Senske–page 72, top left.

The Ohio State University, Austin E. Knowlton School of Architecture

Studio Critic: Bruce Lonnman

First year design: page 13, bottom left; page 70, top right; page 143, top right, bottom right.

Studio Critic: Criss Mills

Third year design: page 26, bottom right; page 69, bottom right; page 78, bottom right.

Southern California Institute of Architecture

Studio Critics: Tom Buresh, Annie Chu, Perry Kulper

Graduate design studio: *Cameron Beasley*–page 19, top right; page 72, top right, bottom right; page 76, top left, bottom left; page 179, bottom right.

Southern Polytechnic State University, School of Architecture

Studio Critic: Frank Venning

Vertical design studio: *Chris Crossman*–page 125, top left; page 126, bottom left. *Clyde Clair*–page 16, bottom left. *Paul Deeley*–page 17, bottom left; page 19, top left. *Ruben Aniekwu*–page 10, bottom left; page 131, bottom left. *Chris Garrett*–page 21, top left; page 48, top right. *Thad Truett*–page 21, bottom left; page 48, bottom left. *Scott Jeffries*–page 125, bottom right; page 130, bottom middle.

Don Son–page 129, bottom right. *Tyrone Marshall*–page 130, top right. *Karin Keuller*–page 131, top right; page 132, top right; page 149, bottom middle; page 178, top left. *Mike Nash*–page 149, top left. *Tony Lois*–page 133, top right. *Bart Stone*–page 141, top right.

Studio Critics: Howard Itzkowitz and Jordan Williams

Second year design: *Scott Fleming*–page 21, bottom right; page 49, top right; page 81, bottom right; page 82, bottom left; page 84, top left, top right, bottom left, bottom middle, bottom right. *Steve Damico*–page 60, bottom middle; page 17, bottom right; page 80, bottom right.

Syracuse University, School of Architecture

Studio Critic: Bruce Lonnman

First year design: page 15, top right; page 22, top right; page 23, top right; page 55, top left; page 58, top middle, bottom middle; page 80, top left.

Structures: page 25, top left, top right.

Tuskegee University, Department of Architecture

Studio Critics: Criss Mills, Patricia Kerlin, George Epolito

Second year design: *Danielle Dixon*–page 15, bottom left. *Allen Pickstock*–page 70, bottom middle; page 126, bottom middle. *Grant Kolbe*–page 70, bottom right. *Dayton Schroeter*–page 71, top middle, bottom middle; page 126, top left; page 176, top right. *Terrance Charles*–page 130, top left.

Studio Critic: Criss Mills

Fourth year design: *Stephen Douglas*–page 69, top right; page 70, top middle; page 178, top right.

Studio Critic: Criss Mills, Jack Ames

Thesis studio: *Leslie Musikavanhu*–forward. *Joaniticka Whitlow*–page 12, top left. *Robert Comery*–page 12, bottom left; page 75, top right, bottom right. *Emilee Eide and Todd Niemiec*–page 48, top left.

University of Arkansas, School of Architecture

Studio Critics: Tim DeNoble, Michael Bruno, Tad Gloeckler and Steven Miller

Second year design: *Arthur Banks*–page 22, bottom right. *Sabina Kruge*–page 23, bottom left. *Juan Andrad*–page 24, top left. *Todd Fergason*–page 169, bottom right.

Universidad De Puerto Rico, Escuela de Architecture

Studio Critic: George Epolito

Third year design: *Luis Cruz*–page 82, middle right; page 86, top left, top right, bottom left, bottom right.

University of Southwestern Louisiana, School of Architecture

Studio Critics: Hector Lasala and Ed Gaskin

Basic Design Studio: *Jason Simeneaux*–page 74, top left, top right, bottom left, bottom

right. Architecture Design III: *Randy Damico*–page 12, top right; page 24, bottom right; page 82, top left; page 83, top left, top right, bottom left, bottom middle, bottom right; page 179, top left.

Design Professionals

Jack Ames, Architect

Page 16, bottom right; page 137, top right.

Robert Bruhns\Jack Ames

Page 126, top right.

Callas, Shortridge Associates

by Steven Shortridge

Page 156, top left, top right, bottom left, bottom right; page 157, top left, top right, bottom left, bottom middle, bottom right.

Kohn, Pedersen, Fox Associates PC

Page 158, top left, top right, bottom left; page 159, top left, top right, bottom left, bottom right; page 160, top left, top right, bottom left, bottom middle, bottom right.

Bruce Lonnman

Page 21, top right.

MC2 Architects Inc.

Page 16, top left; page 17, top left; page 18, top right; page 19, bottom middle; page 62, bottom right; page 141, bottom right; page 142, top right; page 143, bottom left, top left; page 162, top left, top right, bottom

left, top left, bottom right; page 179, bottom middle.

Roto Architects Inc.

Page 163, top left, top right, bottom left, bottom right; page 164, top left, top right, bottom left; page 165, top left, top right, bottom left.

Rowhouse Architects Inc.

Page 15, top left; page 17, top right; page 18, top left; page 22, bottom left; page 23, bottom right; page 64, bottom right, top right; page 77, top right, bottom left.

Scogin, Elam and Bray Architects

Page 152, top right, bottom left, bottom right; page 153, top left, top right, bottom left, bottom middle bottom right; page 154, top left, top right, bottom left, bottom middle, bottom right; page 155, top left, top right, bottom left.

Jack Thalinious

Page 18, bottom left; page 63, bottom middle; page 131, bottom right; page 142, bottom right.

Frank Venning Architect

Page 16, top right; page 176, bottom left.

Venning, Attwood and Kean Architects Inc.

Page 161, top left, top right, bottom left, bottom right.

Photography Credits

Assassi/Productions

Page 165, bottom right, bottom left.

Loyd Bray

Page 152, top right, bottom left; page 153, bottom left; page 154, top left, top right, bottom middle, bottom right, bottom left; page 155, top left, top right.

Benny Chan/Fotoworks

Page 163, top right, bottom left, bottom right.

Susan Desko

Page 153, top right.

Timothy Hursley

Page 152, bottom right; page 154, bottom right; page 155, bottom left.

Steven Shortridge

Page 156, top left, top right; page 157, top left, top right, bottom left, bottom middle, bottom right.

Kohn, Pedersen, Fox Associates PC

Page 158, top left, top right, bottom left; page 159, top left, top right, bottom left, bottom right; page 160, top left, top right, bottom left, bottom middle, bottom right.

Roto Architects Inc.

Page 163, top left; page 164, top left, bottom right, bottom left; page 165, top left.

Frank Venning

Page 161, top left, top right, bottom left, bottom right.

David Yocum

Page 153, top left, bottom middle, bottom right.

INDEX